I0651658

John McDougall

George Millward McDougall

The pioneer, patriot and missionary

John McDougall

George Millward McDougall
The pioneer, patriot and missionary

ISBN/EAN: 9783743345225

Manufactured in Europe, USA, Canada, Australia, Japa

Cover: Foto ©ninafisch / pixelio.de

Manufactured and distributed by brebook publishing software (www.brebook.com)

John McDougall

George Millward McDougall

GEORGE MILLWARD McDOUGALL,

THE PIONEER,

PATRIOT AND MISSIONARY.

BY

JOHN McDOUGALL,

MORLEY, ALBERTA.

WITH AN INTRODUCTION BY ALEX. SUTHERLAND, D.D.

TORONTO:

WILLIAM BRIGGS, 78 & 80 KING STREET EAST.

MONTREAL: C. W. COATES.   HALIFAX: S. F. HUESTIS.

1888.

PREFACE.

TO the Canadian public and the Christians of every Church this humble volume is respectfully presented, the writer apologizing that he did not earlier detail the facts herein given.

The subject of the following sketch was a true patriot, and one of the pioneers of our great Dominion. He was a faithful missionary, and his whole life was spent in the vanguard of Christian work.

That this short recital of the events of his life may stir someone to go and do likewise is the earnest wish of his loving son,

JOHN McDOUGALL.

MORLEY, ALBERTA, 1888.

CONTENTS.

	PAGE
INTRODUCTION	v

CHAPTER I. 9

CHAPTER II. 15

Moves to Owen Sound—Makes business connections—Starts for college—Received as a probationer for the ministry—Is appointed to establish a new mission in the far North.

CHAPTER III. 20

Starts to explore for and establish a mission—Locates at Garden River—His work during six years' residence at this place.

CHAPTER IV. 62

Moves to Rama—Three years' residence at this place.

CHAPTER V. 64

Appointed to the Hudson Bay Missions—Is made Chairman of same – Three years with Norway House as Headquarters—Describes several missionary trips made during these years.

CHAPTER VI. 104

Moves from Norway House to Saskatchewan—Settles at Victoria—Eight years' pioneer work at this place.

CHAPTER VII. 179

Moves to Edmonton—Three years' residence at this place—Journeyings and experiences connected with this new field.

CHAPTER VIII. 201

Visits Ontario—Pleads the cause of Missions—Takes a short trip to the Mother Land—Once more sets his face Westward—Is employed by Government to conciliate the excited Plain Tribes—His tragic end.

MANITOBA AND THE NORTH-WEST 231

INTRODUCTION.

I T is with mingled feelings of pleasure and pain that I have consented to write a few words of introduction to these memorials of a consecrated and useful life : of pleasure, because the task recalls days of delightful intercourse with one whom to know was to esteem and love ; and of pain, because it revives the sorrow caused by the tidings of his tragic end.

Among those whe have "served their generation by the will of God," few names are more worthy of remembrance than that of George McDougall. He was emphatically a man of one work. To carry the gospel to the heathen, to seek out the Indian in his wigwam, and, by the story of the Cross, win him to a better life, was the Christ-like task to which his energies were consecrated ; and having put his hand to the plow he never looked back. Unlike many whose zeal abated in presence of the hardships and isolation of missionary life, he never wavered from his first love, but lived and died an Indian missionary. Hardships and sorrows, in no stinted measure, fell to his share, but he was never known to murmur or complain. The dark side of missionary experience he seldom referred to, and then only to show, by vivid contrast, the power of the gospel to comfort and sustain. In all his efforts to evangelize the Indians he was admirably seconded by his devoted wife, whose name, with his, will ever be held in loving remembrance.

In early life George McDougall enjoyed but few educational advantages, and when converting grace awakened, as it always does, a thirst for knowledge, adverse circumstances gave but slight opportunity to repair the defects of the past. Even when, in the face of obstacles that would have daunted less resolute men, he forced his way to college, the needs of the mission field allowed him but a few months' respite before he was called away to an Indian station. From that time onward his life was one of incessant toil, but by the diligent use of odd moments in his humble home, or by the camp-fire in forest or prairie, he amassed no small store of useful knowledge, and became a workman who needed not to be ashamed. He possessed, as his letters show, intellectual powers of no mean order, while as a missionary pioneer he had few equals, and, perhaps, no superior. At Rama, at Garden River, at Norway House, and in the far West, his name, among the Red men, is still "as ointment poured forth," while his heroic labors and tragic end have embalmed his name in the memory of the Church forever.

Although the greater part of George McDougall's life was spent on the frontiers, and in thinly-peopled regions, yet his days were full of stirring incident "by flood and field," and one could wish that a much larger number of these had been interspersed throughout the narrative. But as the author's aim has been to present a plain, unadorned portrait of the man, he has wisely allowed him to tell his own story in extracts from reports, and journals, and letters, some of which were written with the freedom of personal friendship, without any thought of publication. These memorials will be read with eagerness throughout the Church, and will, by the blessing of God, be an inspiration in missionary effort. They are commended, more especially, to the study of our rising ministry, with the earnest prayer that they may lead some to tread in George McDougall's footsteps, and win a like imperishable renown.

A. SUTHERLAND.

Toronto, *May 10, 1888.*

GEORGE MILLWARD McDOUGALL.

CHAPTER I.

GEORGE McDOUGALL was a native of the City of Kingston, in the Province of Ontario. His parents were Scotch; his father was a sailor by profession, who, becoming connected with the British navy, found himself and his family stationed at Kingston, which was at that time a naval depot.

While George was very young, the family moved into the wild north country of Ontario, and located upon a portion of land near Penetanguishene road, and not far from the Georgian Bay.

Here in the primitive condition of this forest country, the subject of our sketch began really his struggle in life, for, in common with very many of his compatriots, poverty, as regards the things of this life, surrounded him on every hand.

At this time wild and semi-savage Indians roamed the country, wild animals abounded, and settlers were few.

The sailor-life of the father kept him away from his home the most part of the year, which inspired George with the feeling, while still very young, that upon him devolved the duty of bestirring himself for the support of the family. He, though only a boy, cleared the forest, worked on the farm, hunted deer and bears, and in the season trapped the fur-bearing animals, and in every way possible to him worked in the interests of his mother and the rest of the family.

There were no common schools in those days in that country, or if any, only for a short time in the winter; thus George in early life was debarred the blessings of even an ordinary education. All his early surroundings partook of the wild freedom of frontier life.

An occasional visit to the neighborhood of some pioneer missionary who had picked his way across the corduroy road, or had been guided thither by the blaze on the tree, was the only connecting link between these early settlers and civilization; notwithstanding, in the heart of the boy there were yearnings after better things, but the opportunity for his acquiring an education was slow in coming.

In the meanwhile, he became a first-class pioneer; his knowledge of woodcraft became great, he became renowned as a hunter, many a deer fell, shot by his unerring rifle, many a bear was either shot or trapped by him. He could handle a birch canoe or a pair of snowshoes like the natives. Without his knowing it, he was, in the hand of Providence, going through a course of education, which would pre-eminently qualify him for his life work, as this developed.

The following copy of a document still extant, will show how little he knew of ordinary schooling, not as yet being able to sign his own name, and yet, while very young, in stature and in other requirements fitted to do battle in the interests of loyalty and order :

HER MAJESTY'S REGIMENT OF ROYAL FORESTERS.

INCORPORATED MILITIA.

Whereof ARTHUR CARTHEW, ESQUIRE, *is Lieutenant-Colonel.*

THESE ARE TO CERTIFY, that *Private George McDougall,* in *Captain Armstrong's Company,* in the Regiment aforesaid, residing in the first concession, *forty-four* lot, of the Township of *Floss,* in the   District, hath served in the said Regiment, for the space of   *months and sixteen days,* and that he is now discharged from further service in that corps, by order of His Excellency Sir George Arthur, Knight Commander of the Royal Hanoverian Guelphic Order, Lieutenant-Governor of the Province of Upper Canada, Major-General Commanding Her Majesty's Forces therein, etc., etc., etc. ; And to prevent any improper use being made of this Discharge, by its falling into other hands, the following is a description of the said :—

He is about *seventeen* years of age, is *five* feet *six and a-half* inches high, *dark* hair, *gray* eyes, *dark* complexion, and by trade a

GIVEN under my hand and seal at Toronto, this *twelfth* day of May, one thousand eight hundred and thirty-eight.

A. CARTHEW,
Lieutenant-Colonel Commanding.

The aforesaid   thereby acknowledges to have received the undermentioned clothing and pay to thirty-first instant inclusive.

One coat ; *one* cap ; *one* trowsers ; *one* shoes ; *one* pair socks ; *one* shirt ; *one* mitts.

HIS
GEORGE **X** *M^cDOUGALL.*
MARK.

Witness, ROBERT C. STEWART,
Lieutenant, Royal Foresters.

Returning from the war, our hero alternated between the farm and the adjacent towns and settlements, finding employment wherever he could. He became famous as a chopper, and purchased for himself a horse by clearing a number of acres of a neighbor's farm in this way.

In the meanwhile a night school came within his reach. This chance the young man eagerly grasped. In his nineteenth year the grand event in his life took place. He was soundly converted. There were meetings held in a little school-house. One of the neighbors, a Mr. White, who was a local preacher, seemed to have been the instrument in the hands of God in bringing George to seek and find salvation.

Going home from one of these meetings, he entered the house, and his mother and the rest of the children were rising from their evening worship.   They noticed that he was excited; and after a while his mother said, "Well, George, what is the matter?"   "Why," said he, "Mother, I want to tell you, I have given myself to Jesus," and again the good old "Scotch matron" knelt in prayer with George and the others, and together they praised God.

After this, George took his part in the family worship of the house, and presently he is heard witnessing in public, and before long is requested to conduct the public prayer-meeting in the neighborhood.

About this time he became acquainted with a family by the name of Williams.   Three of these, brothers, later on, entered the ministry of the Methodist Church. Association with these Christian people greatly helped George in his new career, and also inspired him with a strong desire for a higher sphere of usefulness. Often have we heard him in later years speak of those who gave him such willing and much-needed help in the days of weakness.

In the meanwhile he became acquainted with an

English girl—a member of a Quaker family who, a few years previously, had come across from England to cast in their lot with this new country. The family's name was Chantler. The daughter was keeping house for her brother, who was running a grist mill at a place called Tollendale, not far from Barrie, on the shores of Lake Simcoe.

This acquaintance ripened into ardent affection, and the result was, George McDougall and Elizabeth Chantler were married at Tollendale, in the autumn of 1842.

CHAPTER II.

Moves to Owen Sound —Makes business connections—Starts for college—Received as a probationer for the ministry—Is appointed to establish a new mission in the far North.

HE was now twenty-one years of age. The same winter George's pioneer spirit prompted him to push on into the wilds of Ontario. On snow-shoes, and pulling his hand sleigh after him, he crossed the Blue Mountains and came to Owen Sound. Here he took up land and formed business connections, and to this place as early as possible the following season he brought his wife.

Their route was from Barrie across to the Notta-wasaga river, thence down that stream to Georgian Bay, and along the coast to Owen Sound. At this time there were three houses, consisting of an emi-grant shed and government employee buildings. There the writer was born. Here father and mother remained for six years, and may be fairly classed among the first settlers of this part of Ontario. Dur-ing this period two more boys were born to them, one of whom died in childhood, the other, following in the footsteps of his father, in his turn became a pioneer in the still farther portions of the great North-West, and to-day is a respected citizen of the commonwealth of Alberta.

Father, in connection with his partner in business, built and sailed the *Indian Prince*, the first vessel sent out from Owen Sound; also later on sailed the *Sydenham*, and in this vessel took the first load of exports from Owen Sound direct to Toronto. She was laden with maple sugar, potash and grain. About this time father had been licensed as a local preacher by the Rev. John Neelands, the pioneer missionary of that country.

Among the earliest recollections of the writer, is his accompanying his father through the heavy forests to a small settlement in the back country, where the young local preacher conducted service in a shanty. His business at this time took him out among the Indian population frequenting the islands of Georgian Bay and Lake Huron, and here no doubt began the life work of the missionary.

Coming in contact with these ignorant and pagan peoples, he tried to impart to them a knowledge of the true God, and already his heart was prompting him to seek his way into the Christian ministry, and thus more fully devote himself to this work of preaching

Christ to the aborigines of our country, and, steadily keeping this in view, we find him in the winter of 1848 recording in his journal :

OWEN SOUND, *December 29th,* 1848.

We now commend our children and friends to the protection of Providence, and to-morrow morning commence our journey to Victoria College, relying on the protection of that God whose we are and whom we desire to serve.

The writer well remembers the next morning, which was stormy. Horse and sleigh are at the door, and presently father and mother having bidden my brother and self good-bye, get into the sleigh and start eastward from Owen Sound to Cobourg, through the boundless forests of old Canada. The object of their journey is that father may attend college. He has been working away through the years, but the difficulties have been great. The migratory and wild life he has led has almost shut him off from any chance to study. But now the opportunity has come, and throwing up his business, he leaves his children with friends, and with his wife enters college. Here we turn to his journal again, and find on record the following :

VICTORIA COLLEGE, *January 15th,* 1849.

Deeply indebted to God for kind friends, and a thousand other manifestations of His mercy and Providence, I would anew dedicate myself to His service, praying for a deeper work of grace.

From another extract we take from his journal, the reader will see that the long-looked-for opportunity for acquirement of an education, by the force of circumstances is nipped almost in the bud. Father barely puts in a term at college.

This morning I leave for Alderville, to enter upon the arduous task of a missionary life, to fill the two-fold offices of preacher and superintendent of the boys of the industrial school. May my grace be proportioned to my day, and by that grace I hope to perform the duties enjoined upon me ; but in every possible way to further that great cause to which I have devoted my life, may the all-wise God make up that which is deficient in me. Amen.

From college he went to Alderville, which was then the seat of a large industrial institution, under the supervision of the Rev. William Case, to whom father became assistant, having a special charge over the boys of the institution.

Here he made himself so useful that very soon almost all the responsibility in connection with the institution devolved upon him, as also prosecuting the adjoining circuit work. Keeping his object before him of becoming a missionary to the aboriginal tribes of the land, he was very much exercised by two things :

one, getting into the ministry, à barrier having arisen in the fact of his being a married man; the other, the field wherein most acceptably and successfully to labor.

In the one case, friends in the Conference, notably Elder Case, rallied round him, and he was accepted as probationer; in the other, the growing missionary spirit of the Church found him the field.

CHAPTER III.

Starts to explore for and establish a mission—Locates at Garden River—His work during six years' residence at this place.

ALDERVILLE, *June 23rd*, 1851.

I WOULD again record my indebtedness to God for His goodness and mercy to unworthy me. During the past two years my labor has not been in vain in the Lord. Souls have been converted, and the Church has extended her influence. To God be all the glory.

June 29th, 1851.—My destiny is the far North, among the benighted pagans. This is what I have long desired, and sometimes dared to pray for, but now that the path is opened, I feel myself to be a little child. Oh Thou Great Spirit, magnify Thy power in my weakness. Do Thine own work.

At this time the northern portions of Lake Huron and Lake Superior were without any Methodist missions, and though Peter Jones, John Sunday, and Thomas Hurlburt had long years before pointed out these fields as being ready unto the harvest, yet up to the present no missionary had been sent.

However, the time had now come. The Conference of 1851 commissioned father to explore this region, and to establish a mission. He accordingly set out,

THUNDER CAPE, LAKE SUPERIOR.

his route being by team from Alderville to Cobourg,
from Cobourg to Toronto by steamboat, from Toronto
to Holland Landing by stage; thence down the Holland
river, by steamer across Lake Simcoe to Orillia,
from thence across Portage, by stage to Coldwater,
then on to the old steamer *Gore*, which was the only
representative of steam navigation in the Canadian
waters of Georgian Bay and Lake Huron.

Proceeding as far as Owen Sound, father left his
family and went on to explore. The following extracts
are from his journal about this time:

COBOURG, *July 8th*, 1851.

This morning parted with the Alderville friends. The
scene was truly affecting. May God preserve His own
people.

LAKE HURON, *July 20th*, 1851.

This morning called at Owen Sound. How changed the
prospect. Nine years ago I was the only member of the
Methodist society, the only teetotaler. Now the Sons of
Temperance are strong, and the descendants of " Wesley "
are erecting a large stone church.

LAKE GEORGE, *July 22nd*, 1851.

The sun is just setting. On the left hand, in boundless
perspective, we have Brother Jonathan's great Western
Territory, a land of forest and plain. On the right, the interminable
mountains of the North. Beneath our feet rolls
that mighty river whose mouth is the Gulf of St. Lawrence,

its shores dotted with the wigwams of that race whose numbers have dwindled away before the "white man's curse."

July 23rd, 1851.—Walked across the Portage and stood on the shore of vast Superior. I have now passed the bounds of civilization. All ahead is both a natural and moral wilderness. May God make me the honored instrument in preaching Christ to thousands of the benighted sons and daughters of these wilds.

Sabbath, July 27th, 1851.—Preached twice at the Bruce Mines, and though severely indisposed, yet greatly sustained in declaring the truth as it is in Christ.

GARDEN RIVER, *July 29th,* 1851.
Have met the Indians in council, and agreed to become their missionary. I have sought the direction of Heaven, and now see the finger of Providence. Oh, Thou in whom all fulness dwells, help me to be more abundant in labors. Amen.

He finally decided on establishing at Garden River, some ten miles from the Sault Ste. Marie. Returning for his family to Owen Sound, he proceeded with them on the next trip of the boat, and eventually reached the destination of the party. He hired a shanty from one of the Indians, to be a temporary home while he should endeavor to build a mission house.

Well do I remember the night of our arrival at Garden River. The whole population, with the exception of three men, were drunk. Hideous yells and noises were around our new home during all the night, and I, in common with all our family, shall never forget the hours of terror we passed through.

The missionary was on the ground, and now his early training came in good. He had some of the language. He was as one of the Indians in his knowledge of the woods and waters. To work he went, both by precept and example. He preached the Gospel, and the Lord blessed his efforts, and soon there was a change.

With his axe on his shoulder, he went into the woods and hewed the logs for a mission house. His boys, with a yoke of oxen, " Whoa-haw-gee'd " them out, and before many weeks had elapsed, he moved his family out of the humble shanty into a large, commodious log building, which in itself was, as it stood there on the banks of the stream, in the centre of the Indian settlement, a preacher of civilization to these semi-barbarians. Here we think it proper to give some more extracts from his own journal:

November 15*th*, 1851.—Nearly four months have rolled away since we landed here. Many have been the vicissitudes through which we have passed. Methodism has now a home and a footing in this place. A comfortable house erected, a school-house well on the way, and all these efforts

3

have been marked with the special providence and protection of God. No accident has occurred. Our meetings are well attended. Last evening the presence and power of God was felt by all. Two out of three of our chiefs were heard pleading with God for mercy.

December 2nd, 1851.—Held the first temperance meeting in this most intemperate place. Tried to impress upon the "red man" the fact that he is a descendant of a race once fearless and independent, capable of enduring the greatest hardship. Tried to point out to them the terrible sorrow entailed upon their people by the use of fire-water.

December 5th, 1851.—Last evening met the chiefs of the tribes in private council at the parsonage, for the purpose of devising means for stopping the bringing spirits into the village. A proposition was made to appoint ten soldier-men, whose business it would be to destroy all spirits brought into the village.

Night after night Gospel and temperance meetings were held.

Other points in the vicinity were visited, and, as to the change effected, let the following letters, written by the missionary and others at the time and on the ground, indicate the nature of the work carried on:

BRUCE MINES MISSION,
GARDEN RIVER, *August* 15th, 1851.

REV. AND DEAR SIR,—In accordance with your request, I write you the first opportunity. I left my family at Owen Sound until I should know our destiny. On the

23rd July, I called at the Bruce; here I was most kindly received—found a society organized, and a young man employed as school-teacher and local preacher. In this capacity he has labored for the last nine months. He receives £100 a year—£25 from the Company, and the remainder from the miners, who subscribe each two shillings per month for the maintenance of the Gospel. Leaving two appointments for the coming Sabbath, I started for the Sault Ste. Marie. Here I met with the Rev. J. H. Pietzel, Superintendent of Michigan Episcopal Missions, to whom I was much indebted for information relative to the missions. He strongly recommended Garden River. On the 20th, I returned to Bruce; met the society in the evening; learned that arrangements were made for the Sabbath, sacrament to be administered, and about a dozen children to be baptized. They appeared disappointed when they understood my position, having expected an ordained agency amongst them. This, however, appeared to be forgotten when I stated the interest taken by the Conference in their welfare, and also the prospect of your paying them a visit shortly. There are in all 120 Cornish miners here, and though the members of society are but few, yet more than half of the above number have once been members. The inhabitants of the Bruce number in all 300.

Sabbath morning the little chapel was well filled, which, by the way, holds about as many as the Alderville chapel. In the afternoon I attended the Sabbath-school, which is purely Wesleyan in its character; the children number thirty-five, with an efficient staff of teachers.

Sabbath evening the village appeared to be present. The best singing I ever heard. At the close of the service, the English part of the congregation requested I should tender their thanks to you for the interest already manifested in their behalf, with an urgent request that you visit them soon.

The young man employed by the miners appears to be useful; yet I think a more experienced person might be more so; at least they want an ordained minister, and without a change in the mining appropriation, they would support one. Money is plentiful. If the young brother could be changed, and taken under your control, it might be better. I enclose the Superintendent's order for books. They want Wesleyan hymns, that the children may use them in the congregation.

Dr. O'Meara (Episcopalian) repeatedly offered his service, but was rejected. Several disgreeable circumstances have arisen out of this.

On the 29th I met the Indians of Garden River in council, and stated to them the object of my coming amongst them. I then left them till evening for an answer. From the preachers at the Sault, I received a note of introduction to a Mr. Church, with whom I found a comfortable home while staying here. In company with this gentleman, I met the Indians in the evening, when the principal chief of this vast country arose and spoke nearly as follows :—

"We are glad to see this black coat amongst us. We hope he won't soon get home-sick. Twenty years ago Peter Jones first, by-and-by John Sunday, afterwards, one Sauh-goh-nash (T. Hurlburt), came to see us; but they all got tired and went away. By-and-by the big black coat sent one here (Capt. Anderson); but they all got tired, not one of them started a school. Two years ago I went to Mont-real; I called at Alderville and Rice Lake, and a great many more places. At Alderville saw the old black coat, saw the Indians were very wise, they all knew paper. Now we want a school. We have sixty children here; they all learn to fiddle and drink fire-water, but not one ever learned a book." This is the experience of one of the oldest, and, it is said, most intelligent Indians in North America.

Garden River is a most desirable location for several reasons; first, there are two hundred and eighty Indians residing here: there are two other bands, the one about fifteen miles up Lake Superior, in all twenty-five miles from here; the other, about twelve miles below this, at the foot of Lake George. Another reason is, that in case of no change being made at the Bruce, I can visit it once a month, the distance is thirty-five miles. Another important thing is, there is good land here, I think not less than three thousand acres. There is another opening at the Munedooning, at Maple Pond.

The Indians are all pagans. Both the land and fishing are good. If the ground could be taken up by a suitable agency, a number of Indians might be collected, as the North Shore tribes have no tilled land. It would be an effort worthy of our Missionary Society, to have at least one station on that vast island, containing a population of more than two thousand, divided into seven villages.

I was disappointed on arriving at Owen Sound, to find that my interpreter had not arrived. I am now on my way to Garden River with my family. Please pardon the imperfections of this scrawl. I make no profession of penmanship at best, but to write on board the old *Gore* is all but impossible. We have had one constant blow all the way up; and I must either send this, or miss the post for another week.

August 6th.—I have rented a shanty which will have to do till a house can be erected. A school might be commenced, but for the want of books. If this want could be supplied by the next boat, we could then commence operations. I have sent an order from the mines for books. They can all be sent in one package. I heartily join the miners in their request for a visit from you. If we may hope for this, I would put off selecting the ground for a chapel and parsonage till your arrival. Asking your counsel and an interest in your prayers, I am, your obedient servant,

G. M. McDougall.

To the Rev. E. Wood, *Toronto.*

Garden River.

Appreciating the deep interest which the friends of Wesleyan missions have ever manifested in the welfare of the native tribes of our country, I have designed to be explicit in referring to the work of God as connected with this distant point of missionary labor.

Twenty months ago I made my first landing among this people, and never shall I forget the circumstances connected with that period. Our voyage from Penetanguishene had been unusually boisterous; and having arrived at our place of destination, we disembarked in the midst of a heavy rain, without house or friends to receive us. The Indians were on the eve of starting for the Mahnetooahning to receive their presents; many of them at the time in a state of intoxication; and we soon ascertained that but three individuals out of three hundred abstained from the firewater. They were, in fact, a drunken community.

My first effort on arriving at Garden River, was to procure a place to shelter us from the inclemency of the weather.

I rented a shanty, but it being unplastered and roofed with bark, was by no means proof against the driving storms. These difficulties, however, were small, compared with others of a different character, which soon presented themselves.

Soon after our arrival here, our village was visited by a professing Protestant clergyman, who, strange as it may appear, spared no pains in misrepresenting our mission, and endeavoring to destroy our character and influence, and, in the midst of heathenism and dissipation, he claims for himself a "holy and apostolic" church, comprising almost the entire community. Believing, however, that God has called us to labor among the people of Garden River, we resolved to hold controversy with no man, but with a humble dependence on God for Divine influence to labor on at His command, and trust Him for the issue, and, blessed be God, notwithstanding the combined opposition of Jesuitism and Puseyism, the good seed has not been sown in vain, but has taken deep root even in this once barren soil. Where once there was dissipation and wretchedness, there is now temperance and comfort. Instead of the dismal clatter of the pagan drum, accompanied by midnight scenes too terrible to mention, there is now heard the voice of prayer and praise. So powerful has been the influence of the Gospel, that most of the Catholics have given up their intemperate and Sabbath-breaking habits; and though many of them do not attend our services, yet a spirit of inquiry is being excited among them, and we believe the way is being prepared for their conversion. Our school, though subject to many drawbacks, has been made a great blessing to many here. Most of the young people can now read the Scriptures and hymns in their own tongue.

We have received on trial, during the past year, thirty members. Many more are almost persuaded. One young man, after enduring great affliction, died in the triumph of faith. Our band of believers, who never before had witnessed the power of religion in the trying hour, were greatly encouraged. The sum of £9 has been given for missionary purposes, and if we take into account the amount of labor which, during the past year, has been given to the mission, it would amount to more than £25.

Last winter the Indians got out the timber for a chapel, 25 by 35 feet, and this spring the building was put up. The society has a property now at Garden River, worth several hundred dollars. It was found to be impossible to work the mission without first erecting buildings for the accommodation of the missionary, as none could be rented. We built a house for the missionary family, 19 by 27 feet, with a kitchen 14 by 20 feet; a house for the teacher, now occupied by the former, 18 by 28 feet; a stable, 16 by 30 feet, and the body of a workshop, 14 by 20 feet.

In connection with the mission premises, we have cleared and fenced two acres for the use of the preacher, and by way of preparing for the anticipated farms, eight acres of land have been cleared, and are now under crop. From the farm we expect much good result. If properly conducted, it will amply sustain itself, and at the same time serve as a means of imparting instruction in agricultural pursuits to the Indians. Such are some of the blessings conferred on, and the improvement made at, Garden River mission. But what is one solitary mission compared with the wants of this vast country? I would that we had the power to convey to the friends of Indian missions a correct idea of the suffering condition of the pagan bands of this country.

Degraded and oppressed by the white man, thirsting for the fire-water, full of all the uncleanness of heathenism, they are fast passing away. Nor are they ignorant of it. Many of them are now ripe for the Gospel. They have long looked to their idols for help, but looked in vain. For the last hundred years they have hoped for help from the Jesuit, but, to use the words of one of the old men, " He brought no heart religion with him." The Indian wants Christianity in earnest. There are strong reasons why they should have it now. Yearly their minds are becoming more and more corrupted by false teachers. Yearly scores of them are dying in their sins, and in their blood.

> "O Christians, to their rescue fly,
>   Preach Jesus to them ere they die."

Difficulties in the accomplishment of this work we may expect. Satan will, doubtless, hold on to his old possessions ; but "the Lord is a man of war, the Lord is His name."

Let the Church of Christ use the means, and hell shall yet tremble at, and heaven rejoice in, the full salvation of this people   Amen.

GEORGE McDOUGALL.

GARDEN RIVER.

REV. AND DEAR SIR,—Our work is encouraging. The Lord is evidently preparing our way amongst this people. Our school is now in full operation, and, considering the severity of the weather, is well attended. The building of the school-house was a difficult task—the snow came on before we got it covered in—yet convinced of the importance of having a room solely appropriated to religious and school purposes, we made every effort. The Indians acted nobly, and, with the thermometer some fifteen degrees below zero, we put in the door and windows, laid the floors, chinked, plastered, whitewashed, and finally had the pleasure of congratulating each other as the proprietors of a comfortable little school-house, free from debt, with the exception of £3, and this we hope to cancel before Conference; for we go upon the principle that it is the duty of all men to help themselves according to their several abilities.

We are deeply indebted to P. S. Church, Esquire, for a gratuitous supply of lumber, use of oxen, and other favors. May the Great Head of the Church abundantly reward him and his kind lady for the deep interest they have taken in, as well as the valuable help they have rendered, this infant mission.

Our watch-night was conducted by the Rev. J. H. Pietzel, Presiding Elder of the Ste. Marie District, and though not largely attended, the night being exceedingly cold, yet it was a time long to be remembered. By the Garden River people, New Year's eve has ever been a season which, above all others, was spent in revelry and drunkenness; but by a number the Gospel has been heard, and its power felt, and old things have passed away, and now, for the first time, these red men, surround the table of our common Lord, and anticipate the dawn of a new year in earnest prayer to the Great Spirit for His blessing. To God we would ascribe the praise.

The good seed sown on watch-night we have been endeavoring to cultivate, by holding a protracted service. The God of revivals was present to own our humble labors. The cry of penitence and the song of praise were heard in our midst. Eleven profess to have received good; most of them heads of families. Some of them are related to other bands, thus enlarging our prospect of usefulness. Intemperance is the great barrier to the Gospel in this country. Could we persuade those civilized and refined gentlemen who sell the Indians whiskey, to stop their nefarious traffic, the work of evangelizing these tribes would soon be accomplished. Chief Chinggwuk can name upwards of a score of his own relatives who have either been drowned, burned, or frozen to death, while in a state of intoxication. Last winter, not less than five women were burned to death in their camps.

Since I commenced writing this letter, I have been informed of the death of a young man belonging to the Sioux band, who, in a state of drunkenness, fell across the camp fire, and before rescued, his abdomen and legs were burned to a cinder. To stay this dreadful scourge of the Indian, we have used every means in our reach—the temperance pledge, the co-operation of the custom-house officers, in preventing it being brought from the American side, and also the influence of those favorable to the cause of temperance. Yet the only sure antidote against this vice is the Gospel; and though a large majority of the people are strangers to its saving power, yet such is the influence it exerts over their minds, that more than half of this vast community abstain, and those that still persist in drinking are ashamed to do so openly. As a proof of this, my family have not been alarmed at hearing the wild war cry for the last two months.

January 15th.—With my blanket, provisions, snow-shoes, —all assorted—and a faithful old Ojebway for a companion, I started for the Bruce. The first day we reached the north end of St. Joseph's Island, and on our way we spent some time with the Pumpkin Point Indians, a band numbering about forty, still in a state of paganism, and, as a consequence, in wretchedness and poverty, but willing to hear the Gospel.

On the 16th we called at Hilton, a young but rising settlement on the north-east point of St. Joseph. Here our way was closed up. The erysipelas, or some disease very similar, had assumed the aspect of an epidemic, and almost every family was afflicted. Visiting all within our reach, and distributing some tracts, we started for the Mine.

St. Joseph's Island, if the mining operations are continued, is destined to become a place of importance; the land is good; almost all kinds of vegetables grow luxuriantly, with a ready market for all that can be produced. Crossing from the island to the mainland, we were caught in one of the most terrific snowstorms I ever witnessed. The drift came flying over these vast fields of ice so thick, that for miles we were obliged to shape our course by observing the quarter from which the storm came. But, conscious that we were under the protection of the Arm Omnipotent, we pursued our way, and nightfall found us quite at home amongst our Cornish friends; and a more off-handed, kind-hearted class of people are not to be found.

Saturday we spent in visiting, and a more suitable time could not have been chosen. Almost every family were afflicted with the disease already referred to; one adult and three children had died, and several others were dangerously ill. On Sabbath, the services were well attended, notwithstanding the cold, for the thermometer stood at 25°. The class is in a healthy condition, Brother Hooper, the leader, is faithful to his charge. The Sabbath-school, under the influence of the same brother, is well supplied with faithful teachers, and is in a prosperous condition.

Here is work for one missionary. A people prepared—
many of them once happy in God; but leaving their native
land and the regular means of grace, they have lost their
enjoyments by drinking into the spirit of the world—yet
still they linger about the courts of Zion. May God speedily
revive His work among them!

I am, Rev. Sir, yours respectfully,

G. M. McDougall.

To the Rev. E. Wood, *Toronto.*

————

[From the *Christian Guardian,* May 5, 1852.]

The letter from the missionary at Garden River and
Bruce Mines, which appears in last week's *Guardian,* con-
tained a very gratifying account of the successful operation
of the mission, as well as the openings for the more exten-
sive cultivation of the promising fields for missionary labor
in that part of the country. The following letter of a later
date, from the same place, will be read with interest and
pleasure by all who love to hear of the prosperity and the
encouraging prospects of this department of our work :—

Garden River, *March* 18*th,* 1852.

Rev. and Dear Sir,—As I have now an opportunity of
posting a letter, and that for the last time till navigation
opens, I feel it a duty to send you a brief account of our
proceedings. Throughout the past winter I have visited
the Bruce monthly. On my last visit I was accompanied
by Bro. H. Pietzel, of the Sault.

On Saturday we held a temperance meeting, when twenty-
five took the pledge. Sabbath was a high day amongst
the miners. God in a very special manner owned the

ordinances of His Church.   Backsliders were reclaimed, and
sinners convinced, and the little church greatly raised.   Five
lovely babes were dedicated to God in baptism.

Before leaving, I received from the Sabbath-school children £1 17s. 6d., as a juvenile missionary offering, and 17s.
6d. from the class.   I was also presented with a purse containing £4 12s. 6d., as a present.   This came in place, for
I had spent considerable in travelling to and from the
Bruce, though I knew not from whence it would come.
Last fall, when the change took place in the mining operations, we had but two members at the Bruce, but God has
owned our humble labors ; we have now a thriving class of
thirteen.

Yesterday I returned from Lake Superior, where in company with Brother Pietzel, we visited several bands of Indians, and spent the Sabbath at Na-yah-mah-young, a flourishing mission, some forty miles above the Sault.   Here they have
a boarding-school in operation, and preparations are being
made for farming.   The American brethren are prosecuting the work with great energy.   Their missions extend
from Sault Ste. Marie to the head-waters of the Mississippi.
How humiliating to the Canadian missionary is the fact,
that while the south shores of vast Superior is dotted with
missions, all in efficient operation, the Canadian coast, with
its tens of thousands of inhabitants, is still a moral waste.

In order that the Indians of both countries may be useful to each other, we have appointed a camp-meeting to
commence on the 4th of August.   A committee has been
appointed to make the necessary arrangements.   We hope
that a meeting of this character will bring out many of the
pagans who will not attend the ordinary means of grace.
As regards personal improvement, though I find my acquaint-

ance with the language daily increasing, yet I have not made that proficiency that I had hoped for.

The first three months after my arrival was taken up in building and other preparatory arrangements. The Bruce requires me monthly from six to ten days. But this, I hope, will be remedied in another year. The miners intend to petition Conference for a missionary, and I know of no place where one might be so useful. I have several times heard you anticipate the erection of a Manual Labor School at Owen Sound.

If this measure could be consummated, and the institution placed upon a footing, so as to receive children from missions in this country, the prospect of educating the youth of these wandering tribes would appear under a happier aspect. The Indians are willing to send their children south to be educated, and appear delighted with the thought that a school of this character may yet be placed within their reach.

Please pardon all imperfections, and believe me, Reverend Sir, yours respectfully,   G. M. McDougall.

To the Rev. E. Wood, *Toronto.*

P.S.—To-morrow morning I start for the Bruce, where I am appointed to hold a missionary meeting on Saturday evening.

Bruce Mines, *March 22nd,* 1852.

The work here is onward. I received seven on trial yesterday. Missionary meeting resulted in £4 2s. 10d., making in all between £5 and £6. The temperance cause is doing wonders.   G. M. McDougall.

GARDEN RIVER, *September 28th*, 1852.

REVEREND AND DEAR SIR,—Your favor of the 16th
instant came safe and the contents were duly appreciated.
In answer to your enquiries as regards the farm, I would
just remark, that I view the appointment of R. Sutton as
providential; his past training will fit him for present usefulness. A tolerable acquaintance with the Indian language,
industrious habits and experience as a Christian will, I
trust, by the blessing of Heaven, make his example and acquaintance with business a great benefit to the community.

The effort towards preparing the farm appears to me to
be beginning at the right end of the work. The prospect
of establishing a manual labour school, as well as the improvement of the Indian in agricultural pursuits, depend
wholly upon the management of the farm. As to its prospects, I believe, if properly conducted, it would not only
meet the attending expenses, but when fairly started would
prove a source of profit to the mission. Vegetables of all
kinds find a ready market at a high price, and roots of the
most useful kinds—as potatoes, turnips, carrots and onions,
etc.—yield an abundant crop. Some expenses must be incurred in providing seed, farming implements and provisions;
for though much can be done towards clearing the land, in
the way of making bees, yet the red man must have some
koo hoosh, pork and bread. Openings for extending the
work in this country are numerous. The Pic, a point once
occupied by the society, is still an open field.

Fort William is now a Jesuit station. To the Indians at
the Pic they have frequently offered their services, but
Ah Tick Rouse, the leader, is faithful to Methodism. I was
informed a short time ago, by a clergyman of the Church of
England, of a circumstance worthy of notice. Some three

years since, when the cholera raged severely throughout the
country, many of the Indians fell under its influence.   On
one occasion, the gentleman referred to was called to visit
two men said to be dying; he found them fast sinking,
but trusting in Christ for salvation.   Upon enquiring, he
found they were from the Pic, and that several years previous they had been baptized by the Rev. T. Hurlburt.
These forest children, though exposed to much temptation,
and surrounded by heathenism, had not forgotten the teachings of the missionary ; and now, under the most trying circumstances, they rejoiced in the hope of immortality.

Maple Point, on the north-east extremity of the Mahnea-
dooahning, is distant some forty miles from any other mission,
so that it could not be considered an encroachment to occupy it as a station.   It is well calculated for a mission, the
land is good, fishing excellent, and the situation convenient
to the steamboat route.   The Indians call for sympathy,
they are at present in a most wretched condition.   Dissi-
pated, destitute and friendless, they are fast melting away
before the Indians' deadliest foe, the fire-water.   May God
move His Church to greater efforts in behalf of these poor
people.   Many enquiries are made about the expected chapel.
Nothing would consolidate our movements here, in the
estimation of the Indians, more than the erection of a comfortable house of worship.   By way of improvement, we are
preparing to survey these lands, so as to designate to each
man his lot.   I have taken the liberty of writing to several
friends, soliciting aid in behalf of a class of this community,
who are truly objects of charity.   I have reference to the
aged and young orphans   Could those benevolent ladies,
to whose efforts the missionary enterprise is so much indebted, have witnessed one-tenth of the destitution that

4

your missionary at Garden River was an eye-witness of last
winter, especially amongst the aged, I believe efforts would
be made to prepare these unfortunates to meet the severity
of the coming winter. Old clothes, second-hand bedding,
would be highly appreciated and thankfully acknowledged.

I could have induced the Indians last spring to have
planted twice the amount of garden stuff, but for the want
of seed. That which had been supplied by a few kind
friends was well attended to, and has yielded an abundant
crop. If the friends of missions would collect a box or two
of seeds, and forward them to the mission before navigation closes, they will confer a benefit on those who cannot
help themselves. With sentiments of respect, I am, Reverend Sir, yours sincerely,

G. M. McDougall.

To Rev. E. Wood.

The speech made by Ojesh Tah, one of the chiefs of
the Garden River bands, in a general council, prior to
the missionary's leaving for Conference :

" Black Coat, I want to say a few words. I want to say
them strong. We want you to repeat them to the Big
Black Coat and Black Coats assembled in council. The
Indians down south have fathers and mothers. We are
orphans. The Great Spirit has done a great deal for them;
He has given them a rich country. He has also sent them
missionaries, who have been parents to them. The Great
Woman Chief has been a mother to them. She has assisted
their missionary in building large schools amongst them,
and in teaching them how to work. They are not poor,
they have plenty of kind friends. Not so with us, we are
orphans; we who live on the north shore of Huron and

Superior.   The Great Spirit has not given us a rich country ; the missionary has not taught us the white man's reli
gion ; no teacher has been sent us, nor school-house built
for us.   We are poor.   We have no kind great fathers or
mother to protect us ; we are worse than our forefathers
were many years ago.   Our forests were full of wild animals, deer, bear, beaver, etc. ; but the white man came and
induced us to kill off all our furs.   He brought his steamboats and large nets, and drove the fish from our shores.
We are poor, and we are becoming more so every year.
Now we want you to say to the Big Black Coats, that we
ask them to help us.   We want them very much ; we want
our sons and daughters to understand paper and to learn to
work.   Tell them that we live in a large country, and that
there are a great many of us.   Tell them about this place,
that it lies between Huron and Superior ; that the land is
good ; that we raise potatoes, oats, turnips, etc., and all sell
for a great price ; but that the Indian knows little about
making gardens.   Tell them we ask for a school, like the
one some of us saw at Alnwick, when we went to Money-
aung (Montreal), three years ago.   We are willing to give
some of the best of our land for a farm, and assist in building the houses ; but we must have the white man to teach
us the way."

The following letter to the President of the Conference, from a gentleman at Garden River, contains a
very pleasing testimony to the good effects attending
the labors of the Wesleyan Missionary amongst the
Indians at that place :

SUGAR ISLAND, OPPOSITE GARDEN RIVER,
February 17*th*, 1853.

REV. AND DEAR SIR,—You will pardon the liberty of a total stranger in addressing a few lines to you, as the subject is one in which, I trust, we both feel an interest, and together offer our mutual prayer for its success, viz., the Wesleyan Mission at Garden River. I became acquainted with the Indians at Garden River in 1846. They were at that time a very poor, degraded, intemperate band of Indians. They had usually done their trading at Sault Ste. Marie, where they obtained the fire-water in abundance. I trust that God made some use of me in benefiting them in a temporal point, as they have, since I came amongst them, cultivated much more ground, built better houses, and began to get for themselves horses, cattle, etc. I furnished them work at all seasons of the year, for which I paid them in provisions, etc.; still much intemperance continued. I long saw and felt they needed a faithful missionary to teach them the way of life and light through Jesus. I hailed with joy and thanksgiving the arrival of the Rev. George McDougall in 1851, since which time God has seemed to crown the labors of this indefatigable missionary with great success. Intemperance is known to only a limited extent. In many houses, where scenes of drunkenness were often beheld, may now be heard the voice of prayer and praise to God. The Indians are very much elevated in the scale of human society, and seem far advanced in civilization.

As to the number now connected with the mission house, I am not informed. The congregation on the Sabbath is very respectable as to numbers, and sometimes quite large, so much so that the school-house is much crowded. The house now used as a place of worship and school-house is one of the most uncomfortable imaginable. Many days, as we have in this hyperborean region, it is impossible to make it comfortable; and as it is not suitable in size, locality, etc., I think it not worth trying to improve by repairs. I cannot but think that the erection of a comfortable and respectable chapel would add to the usefulness and influence of the mission. I am not acquainted with the state of the funds of your Board, but fully believe it worth a strong effort to build a chapel at Garden River the coming summer; and if so, it should be commenced early, as our seasons are short, and not at all times easy to get help necessary for work of that kind.

I think five hundred dollars would be required to build and finish a chapel suitable to the place, with its present prospect of increase. Should the Board appropriate that amount for the purpose, I will contribute fifty dollars towards it, or in the same proportion for a less sum. I understand from Mr. McDougall, there is to be a camp-meeting another summer very near my house, when I hope we may see you, and have the pleasure of your acquaintance.

I wish to say a few words on the subject of Mr. McDougall's salary. I understand that he receives but $320 per annum from the Board. I am satisfied he cannot live at least comfortably on that amount, with his present family. I believe, should you increase his pay to $400, that with such contributions as would be made here, he would be able to get on very well. You may think I take quite too much liberty in making such suggestions with regard to the mission. I do it, I trust, in Christian meekness, as a well-wisher of the success of the work at Garden River.

Though of a different denomination, yet I pray God that much good may be done, not only to the Indians at this place, but also through all this upper country, through the instrumentality of the missionary enterprise.

One word more, and I will have done. I know not what the practice is with the Wesleyan Methodists of Canada with regard to their missionaries. I think, on our side, they too often change them amongst the Indians. It would take a long time, I think, for any other man to get the confidence and gain the influence over the Indians at Garden River that Mr. McDougall has now.

I am, Sir, yours in Christian affection,

P. S. CHURCH.

To REV. E. WOOD, *Yorkville, C.W.*

[From the *Christian Guardian*, April 27, 1853.]

The following letter from the Wesleyan Missionary at Garden River, to Mr. J. Macdonald, of Toronto, giving an account of the destitute and perishing condition of some of the Indians in that part of the country, will, we trust, excite the active sympathies of those who possess the means to supply the wants of the needy. We are requested to state that Mr. Macdonald will receive and forward to Garden River the benevolent offerings of those friends who may desire to assist in relieving the necessities of the poor and suffering Indians of that place :

GARDEN RIVER, *March 2nd*, 1853.

DEAR BROTHER,—My object must be my apology for the present letter. For some months past, I have felt a strong desire to do something more for the aged and afflicted in

this community.   A short time since, in conversation with
the Rev. B. Shaw, Presiding Elder of the Sault Ste. Marie
District, upon the subject, I was informed that they
received yearly large supplies of second-hand clothing,
garden seeds, medicines, etc., from different benevolent
societies throughout the Union.   These, when judiciously
dispensed, not only relieved the sufferings of the destitute,
but also exerted a happy influence in favour of religion.
The Indian makes no provision for old age or affliction, and
when once incapacitated for the chase, his case becomes truly
wretched.

Many of the inland Indians are now in a state of starvation ; the rabbits, which were their main dependence in
winter, having, from some unknown cause, died off.   I lately
visited a band, where one of their women was driven to
such a desperate state through starvation, that she ate her
own child ; and I have good authority for stating that
several cases of the kind have occurred during the past
year.

Accidents often occur which place individuals in circumstances of great affliction and destitution.   A short time
since, within sight of the mission-house, a widow woman
got her camp burned, and a fine active little child roasted
alive in it.   Now this unfortunate not only suffered the
grief peculiar to a mother, but, as regards food and clothing, was left totally destitute.   We believe that were the
right agencies employed, God, through His Church, would
enable the missionary to relieve such cases.   But with me a
difficulty presents itself; for my junior position as a missionary, together with my crcumscribed acquaintance with
persons suitable to co-operate in this work, prevent me from
taking that active part in the work that I might otherwise do.

Trusting in God, however, I have resolved to write several friends on the subject, asking their assistance. Now, my dear sir, if you can enlist the benevolent of your acquaintance in our behalf, you will confer a great favor, and relieve the sufferings of the destitute.

It is necessary to be an eye-witness in order to form anything like an idea of the suffering condition of the pagans of this region. Dissipation, poverty, severity of climate, all combine to augment their misery. As regards our progress in religion, we have reason to be encouraged. Our society numbers about fifty members; and among a people who, less than two years ago, were noted for drunkenness, only one case of drinking the fire-water has occurred this winter. They have raised upwards of £10 for missionary purposes during the past winter. We have got out timber for a chapel 25 x 35. To our Heavenly Father we desire to be thankful, and to ascribe all the praise of our success. Trusting you will pardon the liberty I have taken, by remembering the object I have in view, I remain, yours very sincerely.

GEO. McDOUGALL.

JOHN MACDONALD, ESQ., *Toronto.*

GARDEN RIVER MISSION,
November 25th, 1853.

REV. AND DEAR SIR,—Our chapel has been the object of interest with the Garden River people for the last year. We hope soon to enjoy the fruit of our labor. Christmas is the day appointed for the dedication. The Rev. J. Shaw will lead in the services. The Rev. C. McCulloch, Presbyterian minister of the Free Church, has offered his services.

C. P. Harvey, chief agent for the Huron and Superior canal, the chief engineer, with a number of Christian gentlemen, wish to be present. Should the day be fine it will be one of much interest to the mission, for Christians of every name have taken a deep interest in our humble efforts for the natives. The Indians are not less interested; they have given 145 days' work towards its erection. I hope, dear sir, you will not receive the impression that we are prodigal, because we live up to our income and sometimes in advance of it. I believe there are few families more frugal than my own. The fact is, I have incurred responsibilities in endeavoring to advance the interest of the mission; but we are more than compensated. God has given us many kind friends in temporal matters; and He has given success to our feeble efforts for the good of His people. During the last two years I have received more than $200 from different parties for this mission, all of which I have endeavored to lay out for its advancement. The *Kaloola* broke her machinery three weeks ago. We have no Canadian mail. This is an unexpected favor by a traveller to Detroit; the boat stays but a few minutes.

G. McDougall

To Rev. E. Wood, *Yorkville.*

Extract from a letter from the Rev. G. McDougall, dated January 28th, 1857:

Residing as we do in a part of the country where Popery preponderates, and where festival days are characterized by scenes of drunkenness and dissipation, we have ever looked forward to the holidays with anxiety, especially as regards the young of our congregation. The past, however, were

seasons of pleasing remembrance.   Christmas was a happy
day at Garden River.

Our morning service was well attended.   In the afternoon, with two exceptions, every individual belonging to
the band assembled in the Wesleyan church for the purpose
of enjoying their Christmas feast.   The good things were
provided by the young of our congregation.   The evening
was spent in the defence of temperance principles, and a
most effective meeting it was.   Our watch-night was a
season of deep interest.   How happy the change wrought
in this people, when a comparison is made with the manner in which they formerly anticipated the new year.   On
the 2nd of January, at the suggestion of Mrs. Church, and
at her expense, a pic-nic was got up for the mission school,
and to this, not only the little people, but all their parents
were invited ; every variety was provided for their enter-
tainment—nuts, raisins, apples, and cakes of various kinds ;
and to these you may be sure ample justice was done.

Fifty-four children, and some 150 of the grown-up ones,
were made glad on this occasion ; and, while speaking of
the little folks, I would just remark that, without being in-
vidious as to others, our school is decidedly the best we have
seen in this country ; our indefatigable teacher, Mr. Dagg,
has drawn around him, not only the children of our own
people, but almost all the Romanist children within reach.
Would that the friends of the Indians could witness the
improvement in many of those children.   The class in
grammar, geography and arithmetic, would bear comparison
with most of those of the same age in our favored country.
Intent on doing good, Mr. Dagg commenced a night-school
for the young men, which bids fair to be of much service.
These are some of the lights connected with our work in

this country, and to God we ascribe all the glory, and yet we are not without our shades.

Twenty-five years ago, when a Sunday, a Jones, and a Hurlburt first proclaimed the great salvation to this people, the way was clear ; there were but few opposing influences; but now every inch of ground is contested. Popery, the blight of Christianity, has been aroused to greater exertion since the increase of our mission ; Bacchus is greatly increasing the number of his agents ; not a village, however insignificant, a fishing point or a mine, but has its vendors of fire-water. The holy Sabbath in many places is shamefully desecrated. To meet these soul-destroying influences, and also secure an increase of numbers in many parts of this wild country, a new order of things is about being introduced.

Those points which we now view as distant, such as Michipicoton, the Pic, or Fort William, stand in about the same relationship to the civilized world as did Owen Sound or Saugeen some ten or twelve years ago. Already the tide of emigration has passed the falls of Ste. Marie, and the roar of its waves is distinctly heard on the north shore of great Superior.

Yesterday we conversed with a party already equipped for a journey on the north shore ; they intend visiting Montreal river, and to select a place for a settlement, and as soon as possible erect a saw mill. Many others with whom we are acquainted are looking towards that section of country as their future home. The unequalled fisheries and inexhaustible mineral wealth of that region are the objects of attraction. Now the solemn questions suggested to the mind of the Christian are as to what will be the character of these rising settlements ? under what auspices will they grow? shall the inhabitants, and the sons of the forest, by whom they are surrounded, receive and obey the truth, and be brought into the freedom of the sons of God; or be ignorant of the great Redeemer, and left to their own lusts, and sink deeper into the thraldom of crime and sin? These are questions which must be practically met by the Church of Christ.

Sabbath the 18th we held our quarterly meeting, Brother Price, of the Shawville mission, being with us. Next Sabbath, Providence permitting, I shall spend at that mission. Brother Price has kindly consented to accompany me to the Bruce Mines, at the earnest request of the Presbyterian church. Sault Ste. Marie this winter is destitute of a pastor, and, in connection with Brother Price, I preach for them every third Sabbath.

March 15th we have an appointment at Ma Mas, Montreal Mining Company location, on Lake Superior. In meeting these engagements, we expect some hard beds and cold nights; yet labor is rest, and pain is sweet, because my God is here.

Extract from a letter from the Rev. G. McDougall, dated July 24th, 1857:

GARDEN RIVER.

We have just closed the Lake Superior camp meeting. The weather was favorable, and quite a number attended, and, best of all, the Master was present and souls were converted. Amongst the many that were blessed, two cases are worthy of special notice: the first, a Frenchwoman, a very respectable person, but a bigoted Romanist. On this dark mind the spirit of conviction fastened, and one of the most powerful conversions we have ever witnessed was the result. The lady there and then declared that henceforth neither priest, saint, nor Virgin, should stand between her soul and the all-sufficient Saviour. The next was that of a young man, decidedly the hardest case at Garden River. His father, a valuable native brother, stated that for the last three months he had daily in secret besought the Lord to convert his son. In the clearest possible manner that prayer has been answered, and great is the joy of that family.

We are now hourly expecting the death of a young man, the son of our oldest chief, who spent the last three years at Alnwick School, having suffered from consumption for several months. He is now, to use his own words, " very near home." I was much gratified to hear last evening this dying youth express to his family and friends his gratitude for the kindness and faithfulness of those tried missionaries, Brother and Sister Hurlburt.

A camp-meeting was expected at the Pic. Brother Ash-quabe writes that two hundred and fifty Indians had waited there three weeks for the Big Black Coat. From Brother Blaker I received a letter yesterday, in which he states that thirteen families of the New Brunswick Indians had waited there for some time, in view of going to the Pic camp-meeting. The iron mine located four miles from the Michipicoton mission, has been started under favorable circumstances.

"GARDEN RIVER.

" DEAR FATHER,—Ke-che-me-ticg,—Our minds have long been to write you letter. Our missionary, Ah-Yah-Bans, has often told us that you was the first talk to him to come to this country. We thank the Great Spirit that He put it into your heart. Before this missionary came we all drank the fire-water; we were very wretched; we were very poor, we sometimes worked ; but we gave our money for whiskey ; then we fought. Sometimes some of us were drowned, some were burned to death. Some of our children died while our women were drinking ; and when we were sober, we were much troubled in our minds.

" We have often wished we were dead. Sometimes the Church missionary preach to us, in the morning we went to meeting, and at night we all drink. But now is great change. The Great Spirit has blessed us, most all have put away the fire-water. A great many of us feel the Great Spirit in our hearts, we are very happy ; our young people have learned to sing good hymns, they like to sing; most of them can read the hymns in the Great Book. Last summer Ah-Yah-Bans told us to send two of our boys to your big school. We have just got good letter that they are happy. The Black Coat is good. His wife is very kind, their teacher is the great friend, we thank you for our boys.

" We want to tell you we have a large, good chapel. We helped to make this house. We all worked hard. We were glad when we meet in that house. No white man, but the missionary and the farmer, help us to this house. We think very strange, when we remember how quick the Great Spirit has done so much for our people.

" We like our missionary very much, he is our great friend. We want to tell you little more. We know the white man is strong and wise. We were strong. We not strong now, we become weaker and weaker; the poor Indians want you to help them ; the great chief many times send us wise man to tell us good things, but we forgot them; what we want is religion in our hearts. Send us more missionary, send to the poor Indians all along the shores of our big lakes, then they will become happy, and our children will grow wise like the white man.

"We want to tell you little more; twenty years ago John Sunday, Kahkewaquonaby and Negig came to this country, we remember them, our children do not remember them. Since Ah-Yah-Bans come here, some good Black Coats come to help them.

"We like camp-meetings very much, we will not forget the one at Namekong; we had a great one last summer, the big missionary from Owen Sound brought a great many with him; we want you very much to come and see our country when we have our meeting next summer on Lake Superior.

"We have told our interpreter to write these words.
                    "Your friend,

                         "OGESHTAH,
                         "PAHAHBETAHSUNG,
                              "Chiefs of Garden River.

                         "JAMES ASHQUABE,
                                        "Interpreter.
"*To* REV. E. WOOD, *Toronto.*"

P. S.—The term Ah-Yah-Bans, is the Ojibway for "Little Buck," the name given to father by the Indians, because of his having won in a race with one of their best runners, whose name was "Little Buck," and who at once surrendered his claim to this because of having lost the race.

————

GARDEN RIVER CAMP-MEETING.

REVEREND AND DEAR SIR,—At the earnest and kindly invitation of the Chairman of the District, and the resident

missionary, I made arrangements to attend the Indian camp-
meeting held in the vicinity of our Garden River mission,
and to visit the mission, our most westerly one in Canada.

Anxious to know more of the state of our work in that
region of the country, to witness for myself the condition of
the Indians in the vicinity and region of Lake Superior, and
to contribute in some humble degree to the advancement of
the work of God in that distant part, I gladly availed myself
of the company of the esteemed chairman, Rev. C. Vandusen,
and proceeded towards the most distant of our Indian missions
in this fine province. Fearing a want of connection in the
steamers on our northern lakes, Brother Vandusen and myself
took the route by Detroit, while Bro. Peter Jones, more fortunately, proceeded by the northern route, and arrived at the
camp-ground nearly a day earlier than we. The ground was
well chosen, near the junction of the Garden and Sault rivers,
and contiguous to Indians both of Canada and of the
United States.

Two bands of American Indians, with their missionaries,
were present, and an equal or larger number of Canadian
Indians from Garden River, and other Indian settlements,
swelled the number to a goodly host, such a one as would
at one period in our country's history have filled a stouter
heart than mine with terror.

But these hundreds of Indians of different nations and
living under different flags, met in amity. Many of them
converted, they met as brethren beloved; while all, free from
hostile feelings, met on the ground of a common or general
brotherhood. It was no ordinary sight, a sight calculated
to awaken no ordinary emotions. My heart rejoiced in the
omnipotence of Christianity, in the lovely fruits and glorious
triumphs of Christianity.

There were no whites present save the missionaries and their families, with one or two exceptions. The Rev. Mr. Shaw, Presiding Elder in the Michigan Conference; Rev. N. Calendàr, Presiding Elder among the Germans; Rev. L. D. Price, missionary at the Sault Ste. Marie, all of the Methodist Episcopal Church, were present, and rendered valuable service during the meeting; Rev. C. Vandusen, Rev. P. Jones, Rev. G. M. McDougall and myself, together with Brother Blaker from the Pic Mission, represented Canadian Methodism, and in all our intercourse with the beloved brethren of the Methodist Episcopal Church, we felt that we were one with them. Noble men of God ! may they be more successful than ever in the heroic and martyr work in which they are engaged. We listened with pleasure and profit to the addresses of the brethren named ; and witnessed some of the effects produced by their ministrations.

Habitual as it is to the Indian character to conceal all evidence of emotion, nevertheless the sigh, the tear, the exclamation of joy told how effectual was the Word of God, while thus faithfully preached and accompanied by unction from above. Many hundreds there were of living evidences of the power of the Gospel of the Son of God ; and, during the progress of the meeting, many pagans were induced to give up their idols and seek the Lord "with full purpose of heart."

No case was more thrillingly interesting to us than that of a venerable chief, nearly eighty years of age, and the most influential of any chief in his own or adjacent tribes. For many years this chief had resisted all the efforts made to induce him to renounce paganism and sin, and to give his heart to the Lord. Many of his tribe were converted, and

5

yet he was an idolater. On Monday afternoon, the last day
of the camp-meeting, the rock was smitten, the old chief
bowed in penitence; all night prayer was made to God for
him.   Ere the morning sun shone upon us, the Sun of
Righteousness had risen upon his heart.   He was made
happy in the love of Jesus, and on the following morning
received the holy sacrament of the Lord's Supper, and was
baptized by the Rev. Peter Jones.   During the protracted
prayer-meetings, as well as during preaching, the power of
God was present.   I could not but note that the Indians
in regard to prayer, were very much like some of us in regard to preaching; they were not afraid of being "too
long" or "too loud," yet, whatever might be said of the
preaching, good John Wesley himself would not have con-
demned the devoted or penitent Indians for the fervor,
vehemence or perseverance of their prayers.

Sometimes the meetings continued in the tents the whole
of the night.   The love-feast was a happy season; and
when we parted, never to meet again on earth, "eyes un-
used to weep" were suffused with tears. Few, if any, upon
the camp-ground but wept as they bade a final adieu to
each other.   I know not the number converted during the
meeting; but I was informed that there were many brought
to God.   The result will be seen after many days; but not
fully until the day of eternity.

Before I left the ground, the chiefs present honored me
with an Indian name, Wah-bah-noo-sa.   I was at no loss to
discover that my valued brother, Vandusen, had as much
influence with the western Indians, and he richly deserves
it all, as he had with the senate of a western university,
and that not only to his recommendation was an old friend

indebted for the honorary degree, but myself for my Indian cognomen.

I visited the mission near the head of the Sault, some ten miles from the Lake Superior. It is lovely in its aspect and scenery. A more suitable location could not have been made. The scenery is among the finest I ever saw, the soil is of a superior quality, the streams abounding with fish, and the salubrity of the climate unrivalled. In company with the chairman and missionary, Brother Jones having returned home, we visited many families in their houses and prayed with them there. The houses, about forty, have all been put up, I believe, within three or four years, or since the commencement of the mission. A church and mission-house have also been erected, chiefly by Brother McDougall himself, who is, without adulation, one of the best missionaries in our important work. He is in labors more abundant. Could our friends a thousand miles away visit this mission, as it was my happy privilege to do, and see with their own eyes, and hear with their own ears, the evidences of the wondrous work effected in a few years, they would not only rejoice in having had the opportunity of contributing to such a work, but would resolve to do more than ever for a cause so owned and blessed of God.

I may say, so delighted was I with the evident improvement made by the Indians of Garden River, and with the desire evinced still further to improve, that when a wish was expressed to have a communion service some day, that I pledged myself to procure for them a suitable service and send it, together with books and other presents for the mission, this autumn.

I shall be happy to be the medium of conveying to the missionary there any donation for the use of the mission

which the readers of this hasty sketch may wish to have
conveyed there.

Fraternally yours,

G. R. Sanderson.

Toronto, *August*, 1855.

The reader will now have seen that the missionary
was not content with his work at Garden River; he
went eastward to Bruce Mines and intermediate
points, and westward to the Sault Ste. Marie and away
beyond it. He heard of tribes all along the north and
south shores of Lake Superior; he visited the camps
and saw Indians on the American side; and stirred
up American Methodism by his representations and
efforts for the salvation of these. He was the moving
spirit in the inaugurating of a series of camp-meetings,
to which the Indian tribes came, some thoroughly
interested, others merely to satisfy their curiosity,
but at which all received good.

He succeeded in enlisting the sympathy of his own
Conference, and the Chairman of his District was
authorized to accompany him in visits on evangelistic
tours along the north shore of Lake Superior, where
at different points the Indian tribes of the interior,
for the first time in their history, listened to the
Gospel, and many believing were saved.

It was on one of these visits that the tribe which

Brother Silas Huntingdon discovered in the interior not long since was reached by my late father, and because of his then teaching and preaching to them the Gospel, though isolated and without a missionary ever since, yet, as Brother Huntingdon affirms, they have proved faithful.

It must be some thirty-three or thirty-four years since these men were thus reached by my father. He was ordained at the Conference which sat at Kingston in 1852. He came under what are termed special ordinations.

CHAPTER IV.

Moves to Rama—Three years' residence at this place.

AFTER six years of missionary work at Garden River, father was appointed by Conference to Rama, an old mission, one that had been very much run down by the dereliction to duty of its former incumbent. Here there was not the paganism and crudeness of the previous mission to contend with, but there were as great difficulties in the way of the missionary; these consisting in the fact that very many of the people had backslidden, that very many of the surrounding whites were irreligious and intemperate, and that the facilities for obtaining the intoxicating liquors were more abundant.

Our missionary went to work to face these evils. Not only was his own mission very much quickened and strengthened, very many of the Indians being reclaimed, and a strong temperance sentiment cultivated; but also work among the whites was engaged in by him, resulting, during his three years' term at this mission, in the establishing of two large circuits.

In the meanwhile the Church began to appreciate

him as a missionary advocate, and during the winter
months they called him out into the large centres to
plead before immense congregations the cause which
lay so near to his own heart.   At the end of his term
at Rama, in the June of 1860, to his great surprise, the
Conference appointed him to Rossville, Norway House,
in the Hudson Bay Territory, and also making him
Chairman of the Missions in that distant land.

CHAPTER V.

Appointed to the Hudson Bay Missions—Is made Chairman of same
—Three years with Norway House as Headquarters—Describes
several missionary trips made during these years.

TORONTO, *July* 10*th*, 1860.

THE bearer, the Rev. George McDougall, has been appointed by the Canada Conference of Wesleyan Ministers to take charge of Rossville station, Hudson Bay Territory, in the room of the Rev. R. Brooking, who returns to Canada. Mr. McDougall is also appointed Chairman of the District embracing the mission stations of the Wesleyans at Rossville, Oxford House, Edmonton, White Fish Lake, Lac la Pluie, etc. I recommend him to the Company's officers, to extend to him their wonted courtesies in forwarding himself and family to their destination, and facilitating the object of his mission—the welfare of the Indian tribes within the Honorable Company's territory.

ENOCH WOOD,
Gen. Sup't. Wesleyan Missions,
Canada Conference.

Making his arrangements, and leaving two of his family to attend school in Eastern Canada, as soon as possible after his appointment he started for his new field. The route was by train to Collingwood, for in

the meanwhile railways had been built in Canada.
At this point a number of friends had met to bid the
missionary and his family adieu; among these were
the Rev. Drs. Enoch Wood, Superintendent of Missions,
and Stinson, President of Conference. Receiving the
benediction of these brethren and friends, the missionary and his family embarked on an American
propeller, which took them on the journey as far as
Milwaukee, Lake Michigan, where he and his party
took railway train for La Crosse, on the Mississippi
river, which, at this time, was the most northerly and
westerly point of railway enterprise on the American
continent. Here the party went to one of the large
Mississippi steamers, which were then almost the only
means of transport into the interior of America.

Steaming up the magnificent Mississippi, the mission
party met with the usual experiences in those days—
tying up to other boats for the purpose of social con-
viviality, unloosing and running exciting races with
the late partner; witnessed slavery; saw the management of steamboat employees, which seemed as bad
as slavery; finally reached St. Paul, which was the
limit of navigation at that time. Here the problem of
the big overland journey, from this point to the Red
River of the north, met the missionary. This he
solved by chartering a newly organized stage line to

transport him and his family on one of their coaches
from St. Paul, on the Mississippi, to the Hudson Bay
post, named Georgetown, on the Red River.

The party left St. Paul very early in the morning;
breakfasted opposite where the present Minneapolis
stands, then a few houses indicating the site of a
future metropolis and the greatest wheat market in
the world. The first day brought the party to St.
Cloud, where the missionary learned it would be wise
for him to remain a short time, in order that he might
make connection with a steamboat in the Red River.
Accordingly he camped his party for a short time at
St. Cloud, and, purchasing a bolt of cotton, improved
the time, like Paul of old, by making a tent, which he
and his family very successfully accomplished, stitch
upon stitch (for there were no sewing machines in
those days).

Continuing their journey, the party rolled over
the plains and hills of Minnesota, making passing
acquaintance with the stage-house keepers, and the
few solitary settlers at that time situate in this new
land, many of these a short time afterwards to become
the victims of the terrible Sioux massacre. After six
days' rapid journey, changing horses every twelve or
fifteen miles, the missionary and his party found themselves camped on the banks of the Red River, where

they in a sense entered the Hudson's Bay domain, for here they found a Mr. Murray in charge of the Hudson's Bay Depot. Here the missionary found, notwithstanding his previous stay-over at St. Cloud, that the only steamboat on the Red River was behind-hand; which delay was compensated by the profuse hospitality of the Hudson Bay Company's officer, as also the grand opportunity for the pioneer spirit of the missionary to explore this new country; thus several days passed, and at last the steamboat came, but having arrived, the captain said the water is too low, the boat cannot possibly go down the river again until the water rises. Here was another dilemma, which was passed by loading a barge, upon the deck of which the missionary and his family pitched their tent. Four immense sweeps were attached to this barge and were used as the propelling power. They were now on the famed prairie lands of the far west. Pemmican had become a staple in their food; this was made out of the meat of the buffalo, large herds of which were almost within hearing distance from the banks of the river. They were right on the neutral ground between two warlike tribes; the Sioux on one side and the Red Lake plunderers or Ojibways on the other. The party on the barge kept the middle of the river as much as possible, and were very careful as to the spot they landed on when it became necessary to go on shore for firewood for the cooking-stove upon which they prepared their meals.

Eight days and nights of pulling down the river, leaving Minnesota and Dakota, entering what constitutes to-day Manitoba, the mouth of the Assiniboine was reached. Here the party came to Fort Garry, the capital of the Hudson Bay country, the seat of government of the said Company, and the centre of the Red River, or Selkirk settlement, of the north. Here the missionary and family met with a kind reception from Governor McTavish, and through whose assistance, very little delay was found by them in obtaining transport to their yet distant post further north. Let the following letter, written shortly after, convey the impression of the missionary as to the capabilities and future of this great country:

ROSSVILLE, *September* 17*th*, 1860.

The three days spent by our boatman between Fort Garry and Lake Winnipeg gave us a fine opportunity for observation. We conversed with traders, farmers and travellers on the character of the country; we witnessed the system of agriculture, passed through their fields of grain ready for the reaper, and the impression we received was, that for fertility of soil, and readiness of cultivation, the banks of this western Nile could not be surpassed. It must be admitted that the system of agriculture is very primitive, the banks

OLD FORT GARRY.

(*From a Sketch by Lord Dufferin.*)

of the river often remind one of the shores of the St. Lawrence fifteen years ago, when the French-Canadians either
carried the manure into the middle of the stream, or
tossed it over the banks. This, however, will soon be
corrected. Farming implements are now being imported;
a progressive spirit is being manifested; and the day is
not distant when the limitless prairies which environ the
banks of the Assiniboine will rank amongst the finest
wheat-growing countries of British North America.

And here is a home for the hundreds of sturdy Canadians
who live on rented farms, or who may not have means to
purchase homesteads in Canada. The best of land can be
obtained at a nominal sum.

A word to those wishing to emigrate to this country.
At present we would recommend the St. Paul route. A
through ticket from Toronto to St. Paul by Milwaukee
and La Crosse, costs twenty dollars and fifty cents. A
family would do well to purchase a team and waggon, not
forgetting a tent. Provisions can be obtained cheaper
eighty miles further on, at St. Cloud. The road is good,
feed abundant; and in company with half-a-dozen there is
no danger. In this way, the journey can be accomplished
at a trifling expense. We were much gratified to learn
that the cause of temperance was beginning to exercise an
influence, and that several of the clergy heartily advocated
its claims. On this subject there ought to be no uncertain
sound; the missionary that would be useful in this country
must abstain.

As an illustration, when we were coming down the river
our men stopped at the lower fort, and procured a small
quantity of spirits; singing, shouting, and a great deal of
noise followed. The wind being fair and very fresh, my

son assisted me in the sailing of the boat, leaving our unruly crew to swallow the demon. Subsequently, I conversed with them on the impropriety of drinking.

August 22nd.—Our brigade was obliged to seek shelter on an island opposite Bering's river. Being anxious to visit the Indians, and see the location, we got up a party and went up the river. There were but few Indians at home, and only one of the Company's servants. In Canada we have frequently received gifts from our good-hearted farmers, from the inmates of their sheep and pig-pens; but here we were presented with a fine sturgeon from the fish-pen. The Indians of this location are pleading for a missionary. The young people here expressed themselves as willing to renounce heathenism and become Christians. Though we could not recommend Bering's river as a suitable place for a mission, yet there is a river a short distance south of it which possesses all the advantages of good timber, good soil, and an excellent fishery. Friends of Christ, will these poor Indians have a missionary? We plead for nothing expensive, but let it be said of the Church of Christ that she hath done what she could for them.

23rd.—We are now opposite the mouth of the Saskatchewan, the future highway of nations. A gentleman has just enquired of us, why the Grand Rapids as a mission station has been overlooked. "Here," said our informant, "is the place for active operations" among the Indians. A large body is located there. Past this point all the traffic of the Saskatchewan and the Mackenzie River country has yearly to be conveyed. Now is the time to secure this ground; soon all the important places along this great river will be occupied by the commercial world. Dear Christian friends of Canada, we have no time to enlarge upon this subject, or to plead with you in behalf of the suffering inhabitants of this country. Fields of usefulness there are almost without number, and thousands of precious souls who have never yet heard of the sacred name of Jesus. Now the Indian missionary naturally looks to Canada for a favorable response upon the subject. By the Methodists of Canada almost incalculable sums have been spent in the Christianizing and civilizing of the natives. Through their instrumentality thousands of precious spirits have been loosened from the bondage of heathenism and gathered into the paradise of God. And, Christian friends, what is your command to us, your agents in this distant field? Is it not to go on until the last western wigwam has been entered, and the last pagan brought to the feet of Christ? Yes, yes, blessed be the name of our God, this is what we understand to be our commission, as given us by Christ and His Church.

24th.—We reached Rossville, but could hardly realize the fact. We are now in a Wesleyan Mission House surrounded by old acquaintances; and then to feel that in this vast moral wilderness there is a place where one day is hallowed, and one assemblage convened to honor the Triune God, and to know that the veracity of heaven is pledged to make the little one a thousand. Bless the Lord for all His mercies.

G. McDougall.

The next morning found the missionary and party in one of the inland boats used by the Hudson Bay Company for the transport of their trade to and from the interior. Still continuing down the Red River, the party reached Lake Winnipeg, and coasting along the shores of which, after ten days' voyage from Fort

6

Garry, reached "Norway House." This was the end
of the journey; here was the station to which the
missionary had been appointed. As it was already
late in the season, it became the previous missionary,
the Rev. Robert Brooking, who was now relieved, to
make haste and get out of this northern clime before
winter would set in, which he accordingly did.

Rossville was the oldest mission station in the country in connection with the Methodist Church. James
Evans, Thomas Hurlburt, Henry Steinhauer and
Robert Brooking had labored at this point; a great
deal had been done in the transforming of the people
from paganism and barbarism to Christianity. A
walk through the village, a visit to the church on the
Sabbath morning; a trip with the male population of
this band to York factory on the Hudson Bay and
back; any one of these experiences could not but impress the thoughtful beholder with the fact that the
previous missionaries had not labored in vain; and
yet there remained a great deal to be done. At this
time the Hudson Bay Company were still trafficking
in rum, and this, as always, was proving itself the
greatest bane of the native.

The immediate predecessor on the field had slack-
ened his grip of the people in this respect, and therefore the present missionary found plenty to do; and

A FORT OF THE HUDSON BAY COMPANY.

the Lord was with him in the preaching of the Gospel, in the holding of temperance meetings, in the improving of the church and mission-house, and general material appearance of the mission, in the stimulating of the people to better their surroundings ; he found that in all these lines there was plenty to be done, and characteristic of him he did it, and was blest in so doing.

The missionary's earnest desire to make provisions for the future of this people, will be seen from the following letter written at this time :

To the Editor of the Christian Guardian.

It is generally admitted that the great misfortune of the Canadian natives is their scattered position ; this is not only their weakness politically, and a large additional expense to the cause of missions, but it has also greatly retarded their civilization. The time was when these bands might have been collected in one community ; and we believe had our fathers, thirty years ago, possessed the experience and influence of our Mission Board at the present day, the work of centralizing would have been accomplished. The opportunity for such a consummation is now forever gone ; the fair lands of the Indian have passed into the hands of the " Pale-face," and all Christianity can do for them now is to watch over their spiritual and educational interests. This we are glad to know is not the position of the Indians of Hudson's Bay. What might have been done for the Chippewa, may still be accomplished for the numerous tribes of this country. In presenting this sub-

ject to the friends of the Indian, we lay no claims to origi-
nality; we know that the enterprise has been for years
entertained by some of the most experienced members of
the Conference ; we are also aware that the able Superintendent of Missions has done more than merely speculate
upon the subject.   The good men who founded these missions were not in quest of farming locations ; their great
object was to save souls.   Leaving the rich valleys of the
south, they pushed their way through Lake Winnipeg down
the Nelson River, and finding at Norway House and at
Oxford a wild, neglected people, they applied themselves to
the arduous work of Christianizing them.   Rossville and
Jackson's Bay were not selected because of their adaptation
to agricultural pursuits, but because of their proximity to a
heathen people.   And here we will illustrate the position of
these missions by a comparison.   Our friends in the frontier cities of Canada can boast of the salubrity of their
climate, and the fertility of the lands by which they are
surrounded ; but just suppose a point five hundred miles
north of Toronto, or Montreal, amidst a vast wilderness of
limitless swamps, and barren granite rock—a country that,
for seven months in the year, is covered with a dreary
mantle of snow—and then you have no more than a parallel
to Rossville or Oxford.   In Rupert's land there are millions
of acres of the richest soil ; but the Red River and Saskatchewan are far south of us.   There are a number of reasons
why a suitable location should be selected for the poor
Indians of this high latitude.

The first we shall notice is the scarcity of food, and the
painful fact that the quantity is yearly decreasing ; the fur-
bearing animals are now no longer numerous, and the
rabbit, an animal as necessary to the inland native as the

reindeer is to the Icelander, is very uncertain.   When we lived in the Lake Superior district, for several years they entirely disappeared, and for the last two years they have caught none here.   Fish is the principal article of food in most parts of this country, the hunter and his dog both live on fish ; the quantity required for the winter supply of Norway House and Rossville is 70,000 annually ; about twice that number are destroyed.   Now, all past experience prove that fisheries worked in this way fail.

Thirty years ago the rivers flowing into Lake Ontario were at certain seasons full of salmon.   When the Credit mission was established, it was nothing uncommon for one canoe to take 300 in one night.

From these waters the salmon has entirely disappeared. Twenty years ago, when I first visited Owen Sound, an Indian in our employ by the name of Na-bun-e-qum, caught by the light of one flambeau one hundred trout; I will venture the assertion that last fall, the most expert spears-man on that fishery did not, in the same length of time, kill ten.   Fisheries at all our stations have failed, and the same causes are producing the same results here.   The day is not far distant when the Indian must live by tilling the soil, or perish.   The next fact to which we would direct attention, is the disposition of the native to emigrate south.   Our journey from Red River to Norway, was made in company with the York Factory Brigade.   Ten boats were manned by eight Indians.   A few of these were Salteaux, the princi-pal part were Crees, and most of the latter belonged to the Episcopalian mission.   In conversing with these men we ascertained that many of them were from the north, not a few from our own missions.   The prospect of better land, and a larger supply of food, had prompted them to move to

Red River.   On reaching Rossville we pursued the enquiry, and learned that one-third of our congregation were from regions farther north, some of them from the seaboard, Forts York and Churchill.   They had left the hunting grounds of their fathers in search of a better country.

At present the great centre of attraction is Red River, and the reason is, there is no other settlement in this country to attract the attention of the Indian.   Now, in our opinion, there is not in all the widespread dominions of our noble Queen, a worse place for the native.   A large portion of the inhabitants are French half-breeds, these are all Romanists, and since their country has been opened to the American free-trader, they have become fearfully demoralized.   The Protestant Indian must be provided with a better home.   There is much to encourage the friends of missions in their efforts to save this people.   The Cree, when brought under the influence of Christianity, is industrious. In order to better the circumstances of their families, they willingly spend the summer in making long and laborious voyages for the Hudson Bay Company.   Unlike the Canadian native, he will hire himself out for a year, and faithfully fulfil the engagement.   Only let the Cree have fair play, and he will be a credit to his benefactors.   But we must not linger ; all we wish to do is, to introduce the subject, and then leave it for abler hands to take hold of it. The present time is auspicious.   This country is now in its transition state, the eyes of the speculator and the farmer are turned towards it ; already the pale-face trader and trapper have traversed its plains to the very base of the Rocky Mountains.   Soon its rich valleys will be changed into fruitful fields.

Shall a home be secured for the original proprietors ? or

shall they be left to drink the bitter cup of poverty and neglect, and at last perish as a people? Philanthropists, Christians, you whose hearts bleed for others' woes, we look to you, and may the God of the oppressed speed the right.

G. M. McDougall.

Rossville Mission, *December 24th*, 1860.

During my father's stay at Rossville, he made several trips into the country still farther north, as also westward to the mouth of the great Saskatchewan, where there are a considerable number of Indians located. The accompanying letters will describe some of these tribes, also some of the circumstances connected with them.

Letter from the Rev. George McDougall, Chairman of the District, to the General Superintendent of Missions, dated Rossville, March 22nd, 1861.

We started on the 5th of the month for Oxford.

My kind neighbors, Mr. and Mrs. Sinclair, placed a carriole at my service, but to travel in Hudson's Bay style, I would have to employ an extra train of dogs to carry provisions and blankets. To avoid expenses, I preferred footing it until our load was sufficiently reduced to allow me to ride. In this country when the traveller returns by the same roads, to avoid carriage, provisions for men and dogs are deposited at each sleeping place ; to prevent these from being destroyed by the thievish wolverine, who constantly hangs upon your track, a hole is dug under the camp-fire ; there the stores are concealed, the warm ground covered with snow, which soon becomes a body of ice.

My son, who since our arrival here has taught the school without the loss of a day, gave his little folks a vacation and accompanied us. My interpreter and a young Indian made up the party. The distance from Norway House to Oxford by water is upwards of two hundred miles, by land one hundred and fifty. A few hours after leaving home, we met Mr. Clair, the gentleman in charge of York Factory, on his way to Red River to attend the general council; this we regarded as providential, for it gave us a track, and made snow-shoeing much easier ; and also suggested the question, Shall Britons, in pursuit of legitimate gain, display a greater energy and endure greater hardships than we are willing to do who profess to go forth for the love of the Redeemer, and the extension of His cause ? As the hotels of the north are very similar, a description of one will be sufficient. The traveller selects the thickest clump of trees, in the centre of which he makes his resting-place. After shovelling away the snow, the ground is covered with boughs, a few branches stuck up in the rear, and a fire in front, the roof the one erected by the Great Architect, and the wayfarer's home is complete. Never shall I forget some of the nights spent in this high latitude under these circumstances. The peerless Queen of Night smiled down upon us with a brilliancy and beauty I never before witnessed, while the countless multitude of the celestial host marshalled around their sovereign. These at times are almost eclipsed by the Aurora, which here displays an assemblage of gorgeous forms never seen in Canada. Now shooting forth a stream of silver light, in a moment the color changes to that of a deep red, representing scenes of living fires, while at the same time these different shades are all reflected by the vast fields of ice and snow beneath; while gazing on this inimitable picture, painted by the finger of God, with what joyful emotions does the Christian exclaim, "My Father made them all."

Wednesday, 6th.   We crossed Winepegoosis, a fine sheet of water, nearly as large as Lake Simcoe.   In the afternoon we reached the camp of a large family of natives.   They were all our people, and heartily glad to see us; we all joined in a hymn of praise, and after commending them to our common Parent, resumed our journey.

Thursday, 7th.   This is emphatically a land of lakes and rivers, one portage follows another.   We have seen a few cariboo tracks, and one beautiful black fox; but animals of all descriptions are fast disappearing from these forests. Alas for the poor Indian of this inhospitable clime.

Friday, 8th, was a terrific day.   To give the Ojibway idea, Nan-a-bush-you had shook his blanket, the old giant was mad.   The sun looked pale and feeble through the thin scuds that swept across the sky, the drift was so fine and so penetrating that no amount of clothes was proof against it.   We struggled on until we reached the Oxford River. Here we found a family of the Jackson Indians; they had heard that a strange missionary was expected.   In view of the visitor a fine young beaver had been kept.   This was now taken from its birch-bark wrapper, prepared in backwoods style, and very soon disposed of.   My mind has often been greatly encouraged when visiting those families who, in search of food, spend the winter away from the missions. By them the Sabbath is strictly kept, even when employed by the Honorable Company.   Nothing will induce them to violate the sacred day.   Another characteristic is their deep anxiety that dying friends should give unmistakable evidence of their acceptance in Christ, their last words are treasured up, and reported to the missionary. Most of these wandering families possess parts of the word of God ; in this way the noble James Evans "being dead yet speak. eth." The very simple yet practical character of his sylla- bic letters can scarcely be realized. Not infrequently the pagan procures a part of the New Testament, and learns to read and write in these characters, before he has received the teachings of a missionary.

Saturday, 9th. We reached Jacksonville, and once more enjoyed the fellowship and hospitality of a mission family. Sabbath forenoon we spent among the natives, and in the afternoon, in company with Brother Stringfellow, crossed the fifteen mile portage to Oxford House, where we received a hearty welcome from Mr. and Mrs. Nelson. These kind friends did everything in their power to make our visit pleasant. In the evening I conducted an English service, at the close of which my interpreter astonished his friends by giving in " Cree " almost all I had said, word for word. May the bread cast upon the waters return after many days. Monday morning we returned to the mission. In the evening, Brother Sinclair preached ; and on Tuesday morning we commenced our homeward journey.

We had spent three days with our esteemed friends, and after surveying their field of labor, and to some extent the work accomplished, I feel compelled to congratulate the Society in their having such agents at Oxford. Brother Sinclair has made a respectable acquaintance with a lan- guage that gives him access in preaching to hundreds. With his own hands he has done much to complete their now comfortable church. I was also much gratified to witness the efforts made by this worthy family to reduce the expenses of the station.   When the importance of procuring certain necessaries was suggested, the reply was, How can we spend the Society's funds while so many suffering bands are crying, "Send us the Gospel ? "

Friday, 15th. We reached home, thankful to God for all His mercies.   In two weeks I hope to start for the Grand Rapids, the mouth of the Saskatchewan. This will probably close our winter travelling for this year.

Extract from a letter from Rev. G. McDougall, dated Saskatchewan River, Grand Rapids, July 23rd, 1861 :

Last winter I received three deputations from this people, all pleading for a missionary, and I am now fulfilling a promise made to visit them; having spent a week amongst them, I must hasten back to Rossville ; but next winter, Providence permitting, I shall return, and, with the help of my interpreter and hired man, make the timber for a dwelling-house and school-house.

We must have a mission here, and have already commenced operations, but for the present year shall ask no additional help from the Society.   It would be highly gratifying to you to have witnessed the effects produced by the simple preaching of the Gospel to this poor people.   " It is not by might, nor by power, but by my Spirit, saith the Lord of hosts," and, glory to His name, that Spirit has not been withheld.   Frequently the language of my heart has been,—

> "In these deserts let me labor,
>   On these mountains let me tell
> How He died,—the blessed Saviour,
>   To redeem a world from hell."

From where I am now seated, I have a full view of these majestic rapids. Along the banks of the river the half-naked natives are posted, each with a gaff in his hand, ready to hook out the sturgeon ; the doleful pelican floats leisurely among the eddies, while the black cormorant in flocks are hovering above these troubled waters,—everything indicates that the visit of the white man is only transient.

But what of the future! Once above these rapids, and the noble river is navigable to the foot of the Rocky Mountains, a country for agricultural purposes equal to the best parts of Canada, while recent explorations prove that gold on this side of the mountain is abundant. Several of the Company's officers with whom I have conversed speak confidently of the future ; they all expect stirring times next summer.

Dear Sir, can we not do something more for the thousands of Indians in the neighborhood of Edmonton ? Methodism alone represents Protestantism in that country. From 500 of the Stony Indians the cry comes, " Send us a missionary." This noble band have their hunting grounds in the gold region. They were first visited by Rundle, and subsequently repeatedly by a Woolsey. Many of them have embraced Christianity. We want a practical missionary instantly for this important field.

Chief Factor Christie, of Edmonton, is spending two weeks at Norway House, and having heard that your missionary intended visiting our missions in the Saskatchewan, kindly offers to place means at our disposal next spring for that long journey. This generous offer, the Lord willing, we shall accept.

G. McDougall.

On one of these northern trips, taken in the autumn, the missionary and party came very near losing their lives; they had made a portage, and re-embarking in their canoe, were crossing one of the rivers above the rapids, when an unexpected ripple upset the canoe, and thus the whole party was carried over the rapids.   Father had on his overcoat and was otherwise clothed, so that it was almost impossible for him to swim; but the inverted canoe fortunately came swinging round within his reach, and he grasped one end of it which floated him into an eddy.   In the meanwhile one of the Indians came to his rescue, and took hold of the other end of the canoe, and working for life, they succeeded in getting ashore, just a little before reaching another and far more dangerous rapid. Guns, ammunition, provisions and, in short, every-thing they had in the canoe was lost, and had it not been that a small piece of pemmican which was tied up in a bag, and thus floated on the water, and which they subsequently secured away down the river, starvation would have been the consequence ; as it was, the missionary and his party reached Rossville in a very low condition.

The second summer of father's stay at Rossville, he visited the missions in the Saskatchewan.   The route going up into the country was southward to

Fort Garry in open boat, then westward across the
plains on horseback. The first part of the overland
journey was very tiresome; travelling in the saddle at
the jog trot, up hill and down dale, fifty and sixty
miles a day, was pretty hard on one unaccustomed to
it. The route from Fort Garry to Saskatchewan
overland was merely a pack trail. There were no
ferries on any of the streams, means of crossing having to be improvised at every one of these; sometimes a raft of sticks, sometimes a buffalo's hide,
at all times the traveller running more or less risk
of life and property. Then westward through
Manitoba and onward into the greater North-West,
crossing the South Saskatchewan where the present
Batoche is; touching at Carlton, which was at that
time one of the principal distributing posts of the
Hudson Bay Company in the Saskatchewan district.

Crossing the North Saskatchewan at this point, and
traversing the country lying to the north of this magnificent stream, touching at Fort Pitt on the north
bank, and continuing westward and northerly from
this point, the missionary eventually reached White
Fish Lake, one of the missions under his charge. He
was now, by the route he had come, nearly 1,200 miles
from home, and found himself on the borders of the
great plains of the west and the forest lands of the

north. Both westward and eastward of this point,
the prairie and the woodland alternately give way,
the one to the other.

There was the Rev. Henry Steinhauer. His mission at this point would then be about five years old;
and notwithstanding all his difficulties, he had done
considerable in the establishing of a mission settlement.

Quite a number of Indians had built houses, and
already there were to be found among this people
many evidences of the converting power of the Gospel of Christ. A few days spent at this place by our
missionary were seasons of mutual encouragement.

Then making arrangements with Mr. Steinhauer
and his people to meet them later away out on the
big plains among the buffalos, the meat of which was
the staff of life, the missionary and party continued
their journey, and after two days' travel succeeded in
reaching the Rev. Thomas Woolsey, who was attempt-
ing the establishment of a mission at a place called
Smoking Lake, some twenty-five or thirty miles north
of the present Victoria. Here another of the vicissitudes of missionary life cropped up. The travelling
missionary and party were out of food when they
reached Bro. Woolsey, who, if he had not the same
afternoon killed one of his work oxen, would have had

7

none for either himself or his friends; as it was, tough beef, with very little salt, and without any vegetables or bread, was the only food.

Here arrangements were made with Bro. Woolsey to accompany father out on the plains, where the Indians were congregated, and at which point it had already been arranged to meet the Rev. Mr. Steinhauer. Accordingly father's party was augmented by Mr. Woolsey and his interpreter. The route was now to the south, and the first day's journey brought the party to the North Saskatchewan, where the present Victoria settlement is situated. Here father exercised his authority as "chairman," and instructed Bro. Woolsey to move his efforts to establishing a mission from the Smoking Lake to this point. Camping on the spot, the first difficulty that presented itself the next morning was this mighty river to cross. Here was a mission party without any boat, canoe, or anything else; but the guide soon discovered a way of ferrying his passengers over this rapid-running stream. The means used were these: a large hoop about six feet in diameter was made out of two willows; the only oil cloth carried by the party was then spread out on the beach, the hoop was placed on it, and the corners and sides were turned in on to the hoop, thus leaving the hoop as the rim of the affair. Into the centre of this

ring was put the travelling outfit of the party, saddles,
axe, kettle, frying-pan, guns, ammunition, etc. Several
of the party then, instructed by the guide, took a
hold of the hoop and carried it out into the water.
The weight of the material inside caused it to sag.
However, to the great astonishment of some of the
party, the whole thing floated buoyantly on the water.
The guide now said to the missionaries, "Gentlemen, get into the boat," which they did by wading out
into the stream and stepping into this thing, which
looked like a huge nest floating on the water. The
guide then tied a piece of buffalo line to one edge of
the rim of the queer craft, and catching one of the
horses, he led him up close, and tied the other end of
the line to the horse's tail, and then leading the horse
out into the water, he swam beside him out into the
stream, and the big nest floated serenely along behind
the horse. Father and Mr. Woolsey sitting believingly
in it, the rest of the party drove the horses in behind
this craft, and, each one grasping a horse's tail, were
safely towed through the water to the other side; thus
this difficulty was passed. Stopping a little to let the
horses' backs dry, the party saddled up and resumed
the journey. Great caution was now observed, for this
was the war-path of the contending tribes. Vigilant
watch was kept through the day as the party travelled,

and at night camp-fires were put out and horses staked, and each one alternately kept guard. The beef brought from Mr. Woolsey's home was devoured very soon. A bear and a buffalo were killed; and after several days of travel which bring the party out into the prairie lands of the Battle River country, the large "Cree" camp was reached.

Before proceeding any farther, we will insert a letter written from this point by father to the Rev. Enoch Wood.

BLACKFOOT COUNTRY, *Sept. 2nd*, 1862.

DEAR SIR,—We are now in the country of the dreaded Blackfeet, and in the centre of the great prairie. All around us is strange. One seems to be carried back to some remote, long past age. Never before have I felt so forcibly a consciousness of my own insignificance. Hourly expecting an attack from a war-party, living upon the providence of Heaven, our covering the vaulted sky, our only refuge God—and blessed be His holy name, we are witnesses of His watchful providence over the wants of helpless man.

Our approach to the great camp was very exciting. On the little hillocks that surrounded the little hamlet sat the wild sentinels, each with a loaded gun. Many scores of horses grazed on the adjacent plain. The vast circle of tents, all made of the dressed skins of the buffalo, and many beautifully ornamented, presented a fine appearance. Once inside of the enclosure, and we caught a gleam of savage

life under one of its happiest aspects. The day's hunt had been successful.

Many fat animals had been captured, and stages in every direction were covered with the richest meat. Woman, the slave in all heathen lands, was hard at work, while her lord, robed and painted, sat smoking. An old conjurer fearing his craft was in danger, drummed and sang most lustily. We were received with the greatest kindness. Mas-ke-pe-toon, the head chief, set before us a kettle full of the choicest flesh. O-nah-tah-me-nah-oos, his second, placed his tent at our service. The feast over, the pipe of peace was passed round, and arrangements were made for evening service. How solemn, how burdened with the interests of eternity appears the hour when the Indian herald announced to his tribe the commencement of this first camp-meeting.

For ages these virgin plains had echoed to the hideous cry of the warrior and the dismal dirge of the conjurer, but now they resounded to the praise of the most High God. The appearance of the congregation was deeply interesting. The native Christians collected around the missionary. In the back-ground sat the heathen, their fierce restless eyes and blood-stained faces proclaimed their allegiance to the Prince of Darkness. Yet for these degraded and benighted ones there is hope. The earnestness they manifested while listening to the Word cannot be described. Seventeen times we pointed them to the Lamb of God which taketh away the sins of the world; and our last service was not only the best attended, but, we trust, the most effective. O, God of mercy, have mercy upon this perishing people; their cry, though unheard in Christian lands, is heard by Thee! By many a camp-fire, and in many a smoky lodge, our faithful missionaries have taught these natives the message of sal-

vation, and who can estimate the fruit of their labor? Many
of the pagans understand the syllabic characters, and have
procured parts of the Book of God; and in this way in many
hearts the heavenly leaven is spreading. The head chief,
a fine old man, received a New Testament from Mr. Woolsey last winter. Every day he reads two chapters. He was
reading the eighth of Romans when I visited his tent.

While at the Cree camp, I attended, in company with
my brethren, a funeral. The deceased was a little girl,
and the parents were Christians. It was a sad and mourn-
ful spectacle, and powerfully demonstrated that the dark
places of the earth are full of the habitations of cruelty;
and yet such are the anomalies of heathenism, that men
who regard it a merit and glory to murder a disarmed
and helpless foe, and afterwards subject the lifeless body to
the most shameful treatment, are no strangers to the
tenderest sentiments of compassion for their relatives. The
loss of parent or husband must be deplored with blood. A
finger is cut off, or the arm pierced with a sharp flint, and the
deeper the incision the more sincere the sorrow.

At the burial we joined in in order to prevent the enemy
from discovering the new-made grave. Every effort was made
to obliterate any sign thereof. If it had been winter time,
a fire would have been built over the grave. In this case
the sod was cut with a knife, the earth placed on a buffalo
skin, and after the body was deposited the grave was filled
and the sod perfectly replaced, the surplus earth being removed to a distance. Yesterday Mr. Steinhauer left for
his station. The company of our intelligent and useful
Brother was very encouraging, and often reminded me of
the venerated Wm. Case. By that man of God the Ojibe-
way boy was rescued from paganism and placed in a

position to receive a respectable education, and now, while
the benefactor rests from his labors, the Indian lad is
a successful messenger of salvation to his wandering brethren.   Parting with the Crees was very affecting.   The
native Christians cheerfully supplied us with provisions.
The fierce pagans seemed to forget their natural ferocity, as
one by one they came to bid us good-bye.   The head chief
and a number of his warriors escorted us some distance on
the way.   Farewell, ye simple children of the plains.   May
the Holy Spirit accompany with converting and sanctifying
power the living truths to which you have listened.

We are now on our way to Fort Edmonton.   The scenery
is extremely beautiful.   Judging from the appearance of
these grassy plains, the soil must be very fertile.   Animals
are abundant.   A herd of buffaloes allowed us to pass
within fifty rods without showing fear.   The elegant
antelope bounded past us with incredible swiftness.   More
than a score of wolves were feasting on the carcass of a
bull.   The coyote, or smaller wolf, is frequently seen.
Numbers of whitened antlers, some very large, show that
we are in the neighborhood of the elk ; but the king of the
plains is the grizzly bear.

G. M. McDougall.

Here father met for the first time with the Cree
chief, Mas-ke-pe-toon, or Broken Arm, and was wel-
comed by this hale old warrior to the Cree camp and
buffalo country.   Here were a few Christian natives
surrounded by an overwhelming number of pagans.
On every hand were seen savages in their original costume—feathers and paint and trinkets forming the

principal part of their clothing. In this camp services were held by the missionaries in the open air, and while a number were gathering at the services, the whole detail of savage camp life would be going on in other portions of the large encampment. The conjurer's drum, the gambler's "hi-he-yar," and the winner's exultant whoop can be heard, while on every hand buffalo meat was being handled in all stages of the curing process. Here, without an ounce of salt, thousands of pounds of provisions, in the shape of dried meat, pounded meat, and pemmican, were being cured; this, if preserved from the damp, would keep for many years.

The next day a great hunt was organized by Broken Arm. The missionary and party joined in the hunt; thousands of buffaloes were chased by hundreds of Indians.

Several hundred buffaloes were killed; and the whole party returned to the big camp the same night, having made a successful hunt. Several days passed, being occupied by the missionaries in holding meetings and councils with these Indians. Very many questions were asked. Already Broken Arm and some of the older men of his tribe felt that a change before long must come, and father had seen enough of their country to know that so rich a land could not possibly remain as it had

been very much longer; and he told these men, anxious
to get at the truth, that the day would soon come when
the buffalo would be gone and white settlement come
in. Leaving these children of the plains, the route
of the party was westward and north. After several
days' travel, they reached Edmonton, the head post,
and practically the head of navigation on the Saskatchewan river in this western district. It was now
autumn, and it became necessary for father, if he would
reach home before winter, to make haste. He accordingly procured a skiff, and, having two men, started
down the river. Travelling in this way for several
hundred miles, he changed his skiff for a birch canoe,
and eventually reached the Grand Rapids, and, crossing along the northern shore of Lake Winnipeg, arrived
at Rossville a short time before winter set in. Father
wrote the following letter to the Superintendent of
Missions shortly after his arrival from this trip :

ROSSVILLE HOUSE, *December 25th*, 1862.

DEAR SIR,—I left the Saskatchewan, deeply regretting
that it was not in my power to visit the Stony Indians.
While on the plains we ascertained that they were camped
on the South Saskatchewan, at the base of the Rocky Mountains. To reach that part of the country, and then return
to Norway House before the close of navigation, was impossible. At Edmonton we met with a family of these Indians, and was informed by them that the noble native,

referred to by Lord Southesk in his correspondence with the Church Missionary Society, was killed by the Blackfeet last spring. For years this faithful man had been the spiritual guide of his people, directing their worship morning and evening. We were also told, that since his death the tribe had been visited by the Jesuits, and the priest had offered to place a missionary among them and build them a church.

The chiefs replied, we have been Protestants for twenty years, and though our greatest want is a teacher, we shall wait one year longer, hoping our old friends will remember us. This statement was corroborated by an intelligent officer of the Hudson Bay Company, who has a thorough knowledge of the facts. Assisted by Mr. Woolsey, I wrote them a letter, exhorting them to be faithful, and assuring them that we should represent their case to the elders of the Church, and if permitted, I would myself become their missionary next summer. Here is purely a case of urgent need. Five hundred anxious souls crying for help, many of them still beset with the errors of paganism, yet earnestly feeling after truth.

Yearly they are dying without a missionary to guide their groping souls. Shall these simple followers of our common Saviour be allowed to implore for help in vain? The Stonies have strong claims on the sympathy of the Methodist Church. From the time of William Rundle's first visit they have gladly received our missionaries. Unaided they have translated from the Cree some of our hymns. In many a pass and valley of the Rocky Mountains these humble sons of nature have sung these spiritual hymns of Wesley.

It was on September 9th that we took leave of our hospitable friends at Edmonton. In a small skiff, we commenced our homeward journey of 1,000 miles. Mr. Woolsey accompanied me as far as Victoria. On parting with our esteemed missionary, I found it difficult to suppress my feelings. Friends in the civilized world cannot realize the privations and sufferings which have been endured by these noble-hearted men. Blest in youth with the best of society, favored with the comforts of life in abundance, how great the contrast presented by his present position. For years most of the time a homeless wanderer amongst savage tribes, exposed to all the vicissitudes of Indian life, more than once escaping death by a special interposition of Providence. Herein the fact is apparent, that the Divine approbation has ever accompanied self-sacrificing labor. Many poor Indians have been made wise unto salvation, and not a few, after years of earnest Christian life, have finished their course, and have attained the heavenly rest.

Many were the cheering incidents that came to my notice while in the Saskatchewan. One day, as we were approaching a beautiful lake, my guide pointed to the grave of a chief, and remarked, "That is the resting-place of one of our head men. He was a great friend of Mr. Woolsey's, a good man, and died happy."

Of the lamented chief, La-patack, a Christian gentleman said to the writer, "I spent a week in the tent of the good old Indian, and shall never forget the impression made on my mind by his Christian conduct. Night and morning he called his people together for prayer." But I must not linger. After a journey of fifteen weeks, I reached Norway House on the 6th of October. Nature had already assumed her winter dress, and a severe snowstorm made it very desirable to reach quarters.

With feelings of devout gratitude to God, I review the work of the past summer. From the officers of the Hudson Bay Company I received the greatest kindness, and, without exception, the Gospel has been preached at every fort visited. To William Christie, Esq., a gentleman in charge of the Saskatchewan district, I am under great obligation, also to Richard Hardisty, chief trader in the same district. Through the kindness of these officers these far-off missions have been visited without expense to the Society.

G. M. McDOUGALL.

Thus a journey covering about 3,000 miles, in the saddle, boat or canoe, had been accomplished, and father had seen the country, had visited the mission stations and Indian camps, had estimated the great North-West in some sense as to its value, and had fully made up his mind to cast in his lot for life in this western country.

Being conscious of Divine guidance in this matter, he conferred not with flesh and blood very much, nor, owing to the difficulty of communication with the east, did he have time to obtain the sanction of those in authority as regards his contemplated movements, but went on making arrangements for the moving of his family into the Saskatchewan during the coming season, and for the securing of some one to take up the ground he would vacate by this move.

The latter he secured by bringing the Rev. Charles Stringfellow from Oxford to Rossville, and by filling Brother Stringfellow's place at Oxford with the appointment of a native missionary.

CHAPTER VI.

Moves from Norway House to Saskatchewan—Settles at Victoria—
Eight years' pioneer work at this place.

HAVING secured the permission of the Hudson Bay Company, he took passage with the Saskatchewan brigade in the summer of 1863, and after a long and tedious trip, arrived with his family at Victoria, where he at once joined forces with Brother Woolsey, and took charge of the mission. At this time there was not a building ready to move his family into, the whole party was living in buffalo leather tents ; into one of these father removed his family out of the boat, and then went to work with his accustomed energy to put up a shanty in which they might live. As soon as this was accomplished he started out with his interpreter and one companion, for the western and southern country, and if possible to reach the mountain Indians, the Stonies, to whom Rundle and Woolsey had occasionally gone in the years past. These people had long been without a missionary, and yet with very little light were holding fast to what they knew of the Gospel. Roman

Catholicism on one side and paganism on the other, had done their best to change them, but up to this time, they had remained firm in their adherence to the teaching of the first missionary.

Father was very anxious that before their patience wearied they should again be reached. He had written to them from Edmonton one year before, encouraging them, and holding out the promise that he might be able to reach them before long. Having put his family under the cover of a roof on the banks of the Saskatchewan, at Victoria, he started for the mountains. The whole country south and west of Edmonton was entirely devoid of settlement, not a solitary settler could you find in all that region. There was not even a trading post south of the Saskatchewan river.

A great many years before, the Hudson Bay Company had maintained a post on the Bow River at the foot of the mountains, but this had been abandoned, because of the hostility of the Indians some twenty-five or thirty years since. The party struck south and west, and crossing the Battle River, between where the Battle River and Woodville missions are now situate, and continuing on, crossed the Red Deer river, some few miles west of the present line of road between Calgary and Edmonton. Up to this time, though signs of parties of Indians were seen, not a lodge had been reached. Striking south-easterly from Red Deer, the party came across a trail which they followed ; but which, owing to the autumn weather, and to the dryness of the season, proved to be older than they thought, and finally brought them out again at Red Deer, near what is commonly known as the Big Canyon. Here father met with an accident from the gun of one of his party, being severely shot in the breast and leg ; some of these bits of lead he carried to his death. Owing to the intense pain and swelling of the limb, the party stayed over a day and two nights at this spot. This was truly dangerous ground, being the dividing line of territory between the Blackfeet tribes and the Crees, and the scene of frequent encounters between these two contending parties. The missionary feeling somewhat better, the party concluded to strike back towards Battle River. In the meanwhile, what little provision they had taken with them, was consumed, with the exception of about two pounds of flour. The party was literally depending on their guns for support.

Reaching the Battle River on Saturday evening, every effort was made to secure food, if possible, for the coming Sabbath, and the very first shot that was fired for this purpose received an answering shot from

the thickly wooded hills away to the eastward.
Quickly another shot was fired from the missionary's
party, and immediately there came the answer from
the hills. For many days the missionary and his
friends had been seeking the Indians. This was the
first actual evidence of the vicinity of a human being.

Truly this little party of pioneers were in the great
lone land; and now, upon second thought, the question
immediately came up, "are these friends or foes?"
and the little council in the party came to the conclusion that if foes, they must be numerous, or else they
would not give themselves away by firing a signal shot.
However, the party made every disposition for the
worst, though only three in number. The best spot
was picked, the horses tied up, the ammunition and
guns made ready, and then trusting in Providence,
they calmly awaited the issue.

Presently two stalwart young Indians, who evidently
had reconnoitred the missionary's party, made their
presence known by speaking to us from the brush on
the other side of the river. The interpreter answered,
and immediately they emerged from the thicket, and
plunging into the river, came over. They proved to
be Stonies. With eager faces, and with hearty exclamations of joy they greeted the missionary. The
missionary in his turn was delighted, the object of his

long trip would be consummated; through these men
and their camp he would reach the whole tribe of
Mountain Stonies.

His words of encouragement and advice, as also as-
surances of future missionary help for their people,
would be carried by these men to the different branches
of their tribe in the still farther west, and along the
mountains south and north for many a league would
be discussed around the camp-fire, would be the text of
many a council, and the people would feel comforted
and say, We are not forgotten; the praying men of
the East still remember us, and by-and-by, as they
have often told us, will give us a missionary in our
own country. As soon as possible the Indian camp
from whence these young men came joined that of the
missionary. A delightful Sabbath was spent among
these people, and many lessons of faith, hope and
charity, never to be forgotten, were inculcated. As the
Indians had plenty of dried elk meat, the missionary's
party was relieved of immediate anxiety as to a food
supply.

Sunday evening the missionary said to the interpreter, "You had better take that little mite of flour and
make a cake." Accordingly he shook the bag out on
to another. The young Indian lads standing around
looked in wonderment at this white stuff, and presently

one of them ran off to the camp to tell his people that the missionary had some of the whitest of white earth he had ever seen. Most of this camp had never seen flour, much less tasted bread. The missionary remained several days with these Indians, constantly preaching and teaching. In the meanwhile, with one of them as a guide, they explored the Battle River to its source; his object being to see for himself where would be the best point to establish a mission for this people. Four days of heavy riding were spent on this trip of exploration from the camp.

Then, as the season was far advanced, and the ultimate objects of the trip accomplished, the missionary and his party set their faces homeward, and travelling direct across the country, made all haste for the new mission on the banks of the Saskatchewan. On their way back they passed through herds of buffalo, but turning neither to the right nor left, they found themselves, on a Saturday evening, within about twenty miles of the mission.

Travelling on in the night, they camped short, determining to go on on Sunday morning. Early next day they proceeded on this journey, and had not gone far, when from a clump of willows, the smoke of a lodge was seen; this proved to be old Stephen Ke-che-yees, one of Rundle's converts, whom the missionaries found by later experience to be one of the best of men. The old man and his family were delighted to see the missionary, and without knowing it, he administered a reproof as to Sabbath desecration which the missionary and his party have never forgotten. Said the old patriarch, "You have God's Word, you understand its meaning, you know exactly how far you can go in any matter; all I know is what the missionary told me,—Remember the Sabbath day, to keep it holy. On that day refrain as much as possible from moving camp or doing any manner of work. Now, I understand that, and I don't know any more, and therefore, wherever the sixth day night finds me, I remain until the first day morning also finds me." The missionary sang and prayed with Stephen and his family, and then pushed on to the mission in time to join in service with the people and friends, who were delighted to see them once more. But neither he nor his party, while memory lasts, will forget old Stephen and that Sabbath morning.

Having spent some twenty-one days on this trip, the missionary now saw the necessity of making arrangements for the winter for himself and party. More accommodation in the way of building must be found, provisions secured; to obtain the latter a buffalo hunt must be organized and a fishery established. No one, unless they have passed through the experience, can possibly conceive of the amount of meat food that will be gone through with by even a small party. No vegetables of any kind whatever; no flour, or at least very little, which is carefully put away in case of extreme sickness. The ordinary ration, under these circumstances, at any of the Hudson Bay Company posts is either three large white fish, or three rabbits, or two pounds of pemmican, or three pounds of dried meat, or eight pounds of fresh buffalo meat per day per man.

A full practical knowledge of this was ever present with the missionary, who felt that upon him, under Providence, rested the responsibility of the success of the enterprise, especially, as in his case, he had no wealthy company or government to back him. At best the means placed at his disposal were small; accordingly, father stirred himself to provide for the now rapidly approaching winter.

The first thing was to go up the river, and cut and raft down timber, as also manufacture lumber, every foot of which had to be sawn by hand, which is one of the most laborious duties within the range of manual labor. The next thing was to organize a party, and go out on to the plains for the purpose of obtaining buffalo meat. This was called the fresh

meat hunt. The weather being cold, the plan of
action was to procure the meat, next haul it home;
and then having built a big stage, spread the meat
upon it, and though winter might not really set in for
weeks, yet such was the nature of the meat and the
climate, that with plenty of air above and beneath it,
the meat would keep splendidly for months. Starting
for the plains, the missionary and his party, the
second day out, met chief Broken Arm, their acquaintance of the year before. The old man was delighted
to see his friend back again. Father had intimated to
him the previous summer, Providence permitting, he
hoped within a year to meet him on his native plains
again.

The first exclamation of the old man was, on meeting him, " You are a man of one word. My people
and myself are glad to welcome you to our country."
This fact here illustrated one of the reasons for father's
influence with the red men,—he invariably made every
effort to reach his appointments, to fulfil his promised
word. Storms might come, difficulties pile up one
upon another, long distances intervene, he would put
forth his whole energy to keep his word with these
simple people; and thus, by long years of effort, he
gained their confidence.

The chief, Broken Arm, ordered some of his young

men, the best hunters in the camp, to accompany father and his party on the hunt. These went for the two-fold purpose of assisting in the hunt and of helping to guard the camp, for the common enemy might be expected to strike a blow at any minute; and constant vigilance must be exercised to keep the stock out of the hands of these, the most expert of horse thieves.

On the fifth day out the buffalo were sighted, and every hunter was soon ready, and presently the charge was made upon the buffalo. When on the run after these animals the hunter must of necessity accept the risk of many dangers; the horse may fall, the hunter break a limb, or worse, both horse and rider may be gored by the infuriated beast; a chance bullet from the gun of a brother hunter may strike either man or horse. Then, in the hunt, each man becomes isolated from his companion, and he knows not from which point the ever-watchful enemy may charge upon him.

Cavalry officers who have experienced war, coming upon the plains, and joining in a buffalo hunt, have told me that there is no more danger in the ordinary cavalry charge upon the enemy. Our hunters this afternoon escaped pretty well; one horse is hurt a little, and several of the party have some pretty severe tumbles, but the hunt is, in a great measure, successful, and the animals are fat.

Away on into the night all hands are engaged, working with might and main, in butchering and hauling the meat to camp, for the big prairie wolves, and the smaller coyote, are in hundreds and thousands all around. Three days of such work, with moving camp, in the meanwhile to reach the buffalo; and every cart and waggon is creaking with its load. The party starts for home, and have not gone far when a restive ox runs his heavily laden cart against the hind wheel of the biggest waggon; the consequence is, the axle of the waggon is broken; but father gallops off with an Indian to a hill of timber some miles away, and presently returns with a good stout piece of birch, and in an hour or two a new axle is put in, and on we go.

In due time the party reaches home, the meat is ferried over the big Saskatchewan in a small skiff, the best means of transport as yet. The carts and waggons are taken to pieces and crossed in the same way, and thus, after about fifteen days, the meat is on the stage, and the missionary party, with all their possible dependents, have food for some weeks to come. The next thing is to organize a fishery for the food of both man and beast, for as soon as the snow falls and ice makes, dogs will become the means of transport for

DOG-TRAIN.

the most part; at any rate, all long distances and quick
journeys must be made by these hardy animals. The
ordinary feed for one dog being from one to two white
fish per day, the time of feeding at night after the
camp is made, and the journey is over.   .

Father travelled many thousands of miles with dog-
trains, both in the Hudson Bay region, as well as in
the Saskatchewan country. Two of the little mission
party are sent away to a lake about forty miles distant, and these set themselves about catching fish.
At the time of which we speak, nearly 2000 white
fish were secured ; these, later on in the winter, were
hauled home by the dog-trains, each train taking from
100 to 150 fish at a load. Having made these arrangements, and having in the meanwhile worked in the
camp of Indians, who had stopped for a few weeks
in the fall beside the mission, and then pitched
away again on to the plains to live among the buffalo,
father made several trips, visiting the Hudson Bay
posts and adjacent mission and the large Indian camps,
these trips occupying from six to fifteen days each.
In the meanwhile working with saw and axe, getting
out and hauling timber and lumber for mission-house
and church and necessary out-buildings, all of which
entailed an immense amount of work and planning;
for the place is nearly a thousand miles from a saw-

mill or a hardware store, or any base of supplies; and thus the winter passes.

The blessing of heaven rests upon the enterprise. Each member of the little community is mercifully preserved from the many dangers that surround; for the reader will keep in view the fact that this whole region, for hundreds of miles, is in a lawless condition. Crime of every kind is perpetrated, and, except as overtaken by the avenger, goes unpunished; and yet notwithstanding all this, this little nucleus of Christianity and civilization witnesses the snow melt, and the spring flowers bud, and all is well. Father from the word "go" believed in his missionary career, believed in the broadest interpretation of the word "missionary;" he believed that himself, and everything surrounding his mission, should teach the practical lessons of Gospel life.

Everyone must move, everything that the hand as well as the heart could find to do must be done; the resources of the country experimented upon and developed, and all within his range and capability must be done for the rescuing of these peoples from the barbarism, and shiftlessness, and ignorance, and superstition of centuries, and the removing of the *debris* that lay thick upon them; and the lifting of these, the aboriginal tribes of our country, up into the scale of being that Jesus Christ lived and died and lived again to make possible unto them in common with all men.

In the face of the greatest difficulties he never whined, he never made a poor mouth ; he believed in God, he believed in the missionary enterprise of the Church, he believed in himself; and thus every day, and every hour, found him reaching out and bending every energy to the accomplishment of the grand object he saw before him. During the months of the winter the honorable Hudson Bay Company, owing to the difficulty of transport into the country, and having enough to do to bring in their own material, had intimated to the various missionaries in the country, that they would bring no more material for them, for the time being at least.

This is a new difficulty that must be met. The Hudson Bay Company's boats will come up the waters of the Saskatchewan from their mouth almost to their source; the Hudson Bay Company's carts will roll from St. Paul, on the Mississippi, *via* Fort Garry, across the two big Sackatchewans, almost to the shadows of the Rocky Mountains, but not a pound of the necessaries of life will be carried in these for the missionary ; therefore father must split his little party, and send part of it to Fort Garry in the interests of

his own and Brother Steinhauer's mission. To travel
across the country, to purchase cattle and carts, to
equip these, and load on the scanty outfit for the
next eighteen months for two missions; then to retrace
the long road, with the now heavily laden vehicles,
improvising ferries and mending carts, and travelling
as best you can, takes from the first of April until the
middle of August. This father arranges, and successfully accomplishes. In the meanwhile the Indians
have come in with the spring from the plains. The
whole valley is a busy scene. The buffalo leather
lodges dot the prairies everywhere, the hundreds of
ponies and thousands of dogs mix with the humanity
of the encampment.

Father, and those who remained at home with him,
are endeavoring to teach agriculture as one of the
lessons of Christianity. Some seed has been hauled
by dog-train from Lac la Biche, and from White Fish
Lake in the north, also from Edmonton in the west.
A few garden seeds have been carefully put away by
thoughtful mother. A small portion of turnip seed
is doled out by thimbles full. All the hoes the mission
party can scrape up, and the one plough they possess
are constantly worked, and the beginnings of the mission farm and the first garden patches of the Indians
are the result.

RED RIVER CARTS.

9

The reader will understand that, during the winter, earnest effort has been put forth for the erecting of a building which will serve as church and school-house; this has been accomplished. In this, and in the lodges of the people, Gospel meetings and councils for instruction are being held night after night, Sabbath after Sabbath. Thus father and his interpreter and everybody else around the mission are engaged until planting time is over, and the Indians again take down their tents and start for the plains; for by this time the provisions they have brought in with them are consumed, and of necessity they must move.   The Indians gone, Bro. Steinhauer comes over from White Fish Lake, joins father and his interpreter, and the trio start for the west to hunt up the mountain Stonies and all intermediate people.   Edmonton is taken in on the route. On travelling southward, they strike about three hundred of these people at the crossing of the Battle River.

Some one has seen them coming; who else can it be but the missionary; he told some of our people last fall, God willing, he would hunt us up this summer; here he comes.   The whole camp is astir, the chiefs and the braves and hunters all mount their best horses; the old man of the mountain rides at the head of the column, and thus they advance to give the little mis-

sionary party a right royal welcome. Almost as quickly
as the repeating rifle, in the hands of the skilful hunters the old flint lock is made to sound forth, volley
upon volley.   What cares the thoughtless Indian, that
perhaps to-morrow, or in the near future he may shake
his powder-horn in vain, for no powder is there;
enough for him now his heart is glad, his friends have
arrived, an epoch in his life has come, and he thinks
not of to-morrow.   Years afterwards he will awaken
to the thought that these humble men now approaching the camp of his people have come to make him
think, and cause him to make provision for the morrow.

Such shaking of hands.   Every man-Jack of the
whole party shakes hands with the preacher; then
wheeling into a line they escort our heroes to the camp
in the valley.   Here there is still more of hand-shak-
ing, the women and the children must also touch the
hands of the praying men.   Days and nights are spent
in preaching, singing and praying; souls are converted.

As the missionaries express a wish to see more of
this people and their country, tidings having come into
camp since their arrival that another portion of the
tribe is now several days' journey nearer the mountains, the missionaries and the Indians all move in this
direction.

For three days they travel in company, during which time they have passed the scene of a recent fight, wherein some Stoney boys were attacked by a large war party of Blackfeet. It seems that some of the Stonies were cutting up buffalo which they had killed that morning. Their shots had been heard by the scouts of this war party, and these Blackfeet were now stealthily approaching the unsuspecting Stonies, but fortunately, as was their custom, one of these went out to reconnoitre the country while his friends continued their work, and he in his turn discovered the enemy, and returning to his party, he said to them, "Come, young men, let that alone for a while, here is better game for us." And they charged the Blackfeet and totally discomfited them, killing two of their number and wounding others, and securing their robes, blankets, horse-lines and shoes; for, like all such parties, they were thoroughly equipped for the purpose of stealing horses. Here were the remains of these dead Indians still unburied. Our missionaries took this as a text, and on the ground preached to the Indians the words of our Saviour, "Love your enemies," and practically enforced the teaching by having the Indians reverently take up the bodies of their enemies and bury them.

As the movement of the whole camp was slow, and the time of the missionaries precious, and the distance

yet to be travelled long, father and his friends, taking
an Indian guide with them, continued their journey
and reached the other camp.   Here they went through
like experiences, but under different surroundings.
They were now in the vicinity of the Rockies, and
were actually camped in one of the valleys of the foot-
hills.   For the first time in their lives the missionaries
beheld the grand mountains; the very sight was an inspiration.   Ah, said they, no wonder the Mountain
Stoney loves his mountain home.   Having visited with
these people, having preached to them continuously,
having encouraged the hearts of these wandering men
in the faith of the Gospel, they bade them good-bye
and turned their faces homeward.   By this time the
rivers were high, snows on the mountains were melting,
and many a thrilling experience was passed through
by our mission party as they crossed and ferried and
swam these mountain torrents on their homeward
journey.   By the way they made a big detour, continuing the exploration father had begun the year
before.

Crossing over from the source of Battle River they
came out upon the shores of Pigeon Lake, a sheet of
water covering a space of about seventy-five square
miles, and abounding in fish, on the northern bank of
which they located the site of a mission yet to be estab-

lished, which they hoped would prove a centre for the Mountain and Wood Stonies, as also many Crees. The whole trip had taken about a month. Reaching home, the garden, fields, haying, and many other things occupied their attention. Wandering bands of Indians coming and going, all requiring instruction; applying to the missionary for legislation and medicine. He must be judge, and settle their disputes; he must be doctor, and administer medicine to their sick, morning, noon and night. The work of the pioneer missionary must never cease. The preparations for the winter are as imperative now as last year, and thus the summer and autumn pass and winter has come.

One or two of the Indians have already been seized with an ambition to build a house. The missionary is there to show them how, and though he did expend a great deal of time and hard labor in this style of teaching, yet father felt that he was doing as much good in this way as in any other branch of his work.

During the year two schools had been organized, one at White Fish Lake, and the other at Victoria. Herewith we put on record that father organized the first Protestant mission schools west of Portage la Prairie. The fall and winter of this year were spent very much as last; building, securing food, travelling

from post to post and from camp to camp, getting
acquainted with the people, acquiring a knowledge of
the country, and also preparing for a new mission to
be established at Pigeon Lake. During the month of
March some of the material was transported from
Victoria to Pigeon Lake by dog-train. The wood-
work of a plough, made out of birch, was put together
at Victoria. This was taken up to Edmonton, and
there as a great favor it was ironed by the Hudson
Bay Company's blacksmith, then taken on dog-train
from Edmonton to Pigeon Lake. In the early spring
father sent his son to take up work on this new ground,
and here is another instance of his reaching out beyond
orders. For two years he kept his son at Woodville,
without any assistance from the missionary funds.

Early in the spring he started for the Red River
settlement, the one object being to bring in the supplies for the following year, as the Hudson Bay Company's ruling in this matter still prevailed; the other
was to meet two of his children, a son and a daughter
whom he had left in a school in Ontario, and who
were to come to Fort Garry this season. This trip
occupied some three months of the spring and summer.

In the meanwhile the mission at Victoria was growing. The Hudson Bay Company had established a
post, and were carrying on a large business. A colony

of English-speaking half-breeds moved from the Red River settlement and settled there. All this increasing responsibility resting upon the missionary. The following season the Hudson Bay Company compromised the transport business by bringing the necessaries for the three missions as far as Carleton, thereby saving to the several missionaries more than fifty per cent. of time and trouble.

Let us look into the missionary's house; let us visit himself and wife and growing family. We will be very welcome. Few and far between are the visits of those speaking the same tongue and hailing from the same country as this missionary family. While everything about and in the house is made as neat and clean as possible, rude benches and rough home-made chairs, and very few of these, comprise the furniture. We are invited to take a meal with the family. We see the meat upon the table; grace is said, the meat is served, the tea is poured, but there is no milk or sugar. There is a little salt on the table. We look for the coming of the bread, but it comes not; we would enjoy a potato, or a turnip even, with this meat, but the meal is ended and they are not forthcoming. We are surprised, yet so common is such fare with these our hosts, they don't notice what is a surprise to us. Let us go in another day, and this time we see something

upon the table that we never saw before. Will you
take some pemmican? we are asked. We look in vain
for anything else, and perforce, because of necessity, we
take some of this queer-looking stuff, which we are
told is called pemmican. We cannot say we relished
it very much at first, but we will, no doubt, if we stay
long enough, for our friends and their children seem
to eat it with a hearty good-will. We go in another
day, and we gather with the family around the board,
and, to our great astonishment, a great big dish filled
with boiled eggs is put upon the table. "I am sorry
we have not anything else," is the humble apology of
our hostess. We eat eggs and eggs until we have
enough. We come along another time, and, having
travelled far, are hungry. As before, we are welcome
to this hospitable table. A big plate of potatoes is
put before us, and some milk is poured out and placed
beside us. Again we are told, "We are sorry there is
nothing else in the house." Yet another time we reach
this pioneer home, and a big dish of boiled fish is put
upon the table, and we are asked to make our meal of
fish, sometimes with salt, sometimes without it. Such
were the constant and ever recurring experiences of
the people who lived in this land in those days.

Did the patient mother ever utter a word of complaint? No! We have already said the father was

never known to whine, and as like begets like, there is very little complaint among the children. Sometimes there is very little of anything, and sometimes dire hunger makes the little ones cry out. Gradually the missionary is working his way to a better state of things, but this takes time and long years of patient endeavor. Many are those depending upon him. The weary traveller, who never is turned away; the starving families and camps of Indians, who fall back upon the mission as their house of refuge; all these handicap him in his struggling upward—we mean material climbing, for spiritually such experiences are as wings lent wherewith heavenward to fly.

During the next winter father works hard among this people, visits the Indian camps far and near, takes a trip with old Broken Arm and a large following of Crees out into the Blackfoot country, and is instrumental in effecting a peace with the enemy, which gives the whole country for some months a respite from the terrors of war. Some three weeks were spent on this trip, and a great many Indian camps visited in the meanwhile. With spring comes the stirring up of the people by the missionary to agriculture. In doing this he must take the lead, he must furnish the seed, he must set the example in his own field.

Anyone visiting the chairman of this immense district, reaching from the Hudson Bay to the Rocky Mountains, and from the boundary line as far north as you can go, would have hardly recognized him, except that they saw the one white man among a crowd of Indians. Coat and waistcoat off, up to his eyes in work, from morning until night; this was the daily experience of father at these times.

Farming, doctoring, law making, teaching, preaching; truly his duties were legion. The following summer the monotony of this life was varied. The report comes to the mission that his son, the one that is breaking in for mission work at Pigeon Lake, and who has gone out with a small camp of Indians into the Blackfoot country, is lost. Again the report is different, " he is killed," and father organized a little party, and starts out to make sure. To his great joy, he meets his boy when he is about 120 miles from home, coming in with the party loaded with provisions for the coming winter.

In a country where there are but few men to spare, the reader will readily imagine the experiences of those few weeks to these fond parents and friends. Other matters now demand father's attention. His family has grown. Three daughters are ready for school, and there is none in the country. The work is growing.

Some parts of this district want re-manning, and other points should be taken up. Often has he written; but we are so far off, that the written cry for help loses its emphasis before it reaches its destination. Accordingly he makes up his mind to start for Eastern Canada.

Making his arrangements, and bidding a portion of his family good-bye, he takes three girls with him, and another, whose father also is anxious she should be educated. With two Indian boys as his help, father started as the summer was waning, and drove the 1,800 miles across the big plains of the North-West and Minnesota to St. Paul, on the Mississippi. Here he placed his two Indian boys with farmers to learn some of the arts of civilization during the winter months. Continuing his journey, he reached Ontario. Putting his children to school in the Wesleyan Female College at Hamilton, he became subject to the Missionary Secretary, and travelled the country in the interests of missions; and, as very many Canadians will remember, awakening them for the first time to a knowledge of this immense country.

On previous visits to the Red River settlement, as also on his way down this time, father had noted with sorrow the fact that the Methodist Church was not represented in the whole Red River country. Our

missions were north and west, but in this, which he
very well knew was, geographically, placed by Him
who created it to become a radiating centre, there was
not even a solitary Methodist preacher. He had
written about it, and now he was going to speak
about it. His importunity produced results, and we
see him the next summer leaving Ontario at the head
of a party of missionaries and teachers for Red River
and the country to the north-west of it.

He brought with him the Rev. G. Young, whose
history in connection with Manitoba, Canadians are
proud of. If Methodism has done anything for Manitoba and the North-West; if Methodism is an established fact in the growth and make-up of this developing country; we claim that to father falls the honor of
inaugurating this work.

He had with him Egerton R. Young, who spent
eight years of zealous missionary toil at Norway
House and Beren's River; also Peter Campbell, who
labored for five years on the Saskatchewan, and whom
the Indians remember and speak of with respect and
friendship as " Blackhead," because of his coal-black
hair. He had with him the two Snyder brothers, who
for some years taught schools on the Saskatchewan,
one of whom is to-day an honored minister in the
London Conference. It took a long time to travel

from the Mississippi by waggon and cart, and these heavily laden, to Fort Garry, and the 1,000 miles beyond it, on to the Upper Saskatchewan, but early autumn saw each and all at work in their respective fields. A winter in Canada had but stirred to greater heat the missionary heart of our father. The same fall, after his return, he visited his son at Pigeon Lake. Many of the Indians before his arrival pitched away into the timber countries of the North-West. In these camps that had gone away there were some people who wished for Christian marriage.

There were also a number of children, whose parents desired for them Christian baptism. The night of father's arrival at Pigeon Lake, the people there were gathered for service. Father addressed them, and a blessing rested upon the meeting. After the meeting the young missionary spoke of the camp that had already gone into the thickets and muskegs, which lie away to the North-West. "Let us follow them up," said father, and the next morning away went the party on the trail of the hunting camp. The third day the missionary party came up with the Indians. No one could imagine how delighted these people were to see the old missionary. Glorious meetings were held in that camp, and the writer can think of quite a number whom he believes are in heaven to-day as the result of that visit.

Through with this work, we started on the homeward journey. The first night out from the Indian camp father had a dream. He had been talking about a mutual friend, a man who was once a minister in the Methodist Church. This man had gone up that fall into the Lac la Biche country, and father had said to me, "I am anxious about Mr. Connor ; he is very energetic, but at times very rash also."

Well, this night father dreamed that Mr. Connor had been drowned. He told me of it the following morning as we were eating our breakfast in the camp, and to my surprise, and to his also, on his way home, at Edmonton he met with the news, and writing to me from this point, said : " How strange that I should have dreamed about Connor as I did. To-day I have heard that he is actually drowned." The place where he dreamed was 280 miles from the locality where our friend had lost his life. I will say here, that I never in all my recollection knew a man further removed from superstition of any nature than father was.

The following winter was one of hard experiences all over the Saskatchewan country. The buffalo left the region and went south. The mission family at

Victoria fared hard in common with the rest. Our missionaries, with their people, organized a general hunt the following spring.

This was to be turned, as much as possible, into the shape of a camp-meeting. In those days the only place where large companies could congregate for any length of time was in the vicinity of the big herds of buffalo, as no other food supply in the country would be adequate. While this was being organized, and as the spring opened up, the sad tidings came in from the plains that Broken Arm had been killed. The old chief, the white man's friend, the man who worked harder in the interests of peace than any other Indian in the whole country, and who now, with a flag of truce in his hand, was negotiating peace with the Blackfeet, had been treacherously shot by them. The savages had cut the old man to pieces, and had dragged his remains at the tails of their horses into their camp.

Our hearts were sad because of the loss of Broken Arm, and, moreover, we knew that the coming season would be one of intense hostility between the tribes. Vengeance would demand it. However, from each mission both missionary and people, immediately the spring work of seeding had been done, started for the rendezvous on the plains. This point was about 200

10

miles southeast of Victoria. The objects, for the most
part, were accomplished. Provisions were made, the
people from the different localities of the country
became acquainted with each other. This tended to
break up old feuds, and to enlighten the people as to
the population of their own country. Gospel meetings
were held, the word was faithfully preached by the
various missionaries, and this famous gathering on the
plains is often referred to by the Indians and half-
breeds all over the country.

Here we will insert a letter written by father within
a few months of this gathering, which will also continue the narrative in the subsequent experiences of
the season, and will explain the state of the country
at that time.

It was during this summer that quite a number of
horses were stolen from the mission and its vicinity
by the Blackfeet.

To REV. DR. WOOD, Methodist Mission Rooms, *Toronto.*

I wrote you in August, giving a brief account of a nine
weeks' journey in the plains. Since that date we have had
no communication with the frontier world, and now expect
none until January. Our spring hunt was a success. In a
camp of one thousand people, five thousand buffalo were
slaughtered ; and one hundred and twenty thousand pounds
of dried meat secured. All felt that if our crops should be
as abundant as in years past, there would be no starvation

for some years to come ; but there was room for anxiety. Two hundred miles from the Saskatchewan, scarcely any rain had fallen. The oldest in the camp had never witnessed the like before.

The rich valleys hitherto encumbered with vegetation are now parched and burnt. Fifty miles south of Victoria we met parties who informed us that our fields were a failure. The seed had dried up in the earth. This was sad news. The season was too far advanced to send to Red River. Benton is much nearer, but between us and that place the merciless Blackfeet ranges the plains. There was but one course open, and that was to strike for the buffalo country. For months we had lived on flesh and fowl, and for eighteen months to come we have no prospect of a change. A council was held, and it was determined that as soon as our animals were rested we should return to the hunt. In the meantime, the Blackfeet made a raid upon Victoria, and some of our people suffered severely. Since the murder of our lamented chief, the Crees have killed nearly one hundred Blackfeet, and in retaliation the enemy has resolved to carry the war into the Cree country. They have sent us word that they have spotted the Company's posts on the Saskatchewan, and in particular Victoria. Pray for us. Our dangers and difficulties at times are almost insurmountable. We deeply feel that nothing but an ardent love for souls, and a strong trust in God's mighty power, not only to save, but to restrain, will carry us through these times.

August 16th.—Starting for the plains.

In old times crossing the river with a large camp was a tedious affair, and to the uninitiated trying to the nerves. A leather tent, or, as in my own case, an oil-cloth, was spread on the beach, the travelling kit was placed in the centre, then the cloth gathered up and tied at the top, giving the appearance of a huge pudding-bag. The raft is then shoved into the water, and attached by a line to a horse's tail; the traveller then mounts the boat and guides the swimming steed to the opposite shore. In this way and in a very short time, I have crossed large rivers. We have now a good scow, and the novel scenes of yore have passed away.

August 18*th.*—For years pemmican has been the staple dish on our table, yet I must confess, I have very little relish for tallow and pounded meat. My wife says that it is better not to think of bread, while we cannot have it, as the thought might cause impatience. I shall not controvert her opinion, but judging from my feelings this morning, *the sight of a four pound loaf* would produce in my poor heart the liveliest gratitude.

With my horse and gun, I shall leave the brigade to move on, hoping to join them in the evening with something fresh for supper. A little while before sundown I reached a round hill that rises about three hundred feet above the level of the plain. From the top of this little mountain the magnificence and profusion of the prairie met the eye. The silence and solitude is overwhelming, and this feeling increases with the conviction that we have only entered into the vestibule of Nature's great temple; for this is but the margin of the plains, and now, the mirage adds to the beauty of the bewildering panorama. In a moment the little lakes appear above the plains, and the distant bluffs of aspen dance in mid-air. From these majestic scenes the untutored Indian paints his future paradise. Alas for him, his religion makes his heart no better; yet, however steeped in sensuality or stained with blood, the native loves nature. He will sit for hours on the hill-top, and gaze with placid satisfaction on the wild and beautiful. Thank the Lord, we have now both Crees and Stonies who look from nature to nature's God, and with joyful hearts they worship the Creator who is blessed forever.

August 20th, Sabbath.—Our services are still well attended, and the holy day sacredly kept. This is our sowing time. We shall reap if we faint not. On the plains there is much to divide the attention ; the stock must be guarded, and there is a constant dread of an attack from the enemy.

After the morning service we were informed that a stranger had entered the camp under suspicious circumstances. The rider had no saddle. A cold rain was falling, but the fugitive was naked. When questioned, his answers were evasive, until a Christian woman took him into her tent, gave him her son's coat, and placed food before him. Kindness prevailed, and he stated that yesterday before dawn he started with his companions, hoping to find game, and while crawling through the brush he saw something black, and thinking it was a bear, fired, when a woman threw up her arms and cried out, "I am killed ! I am killed !" She was one of the party ahead of us, who, in company with her sister, had gone into the woods in search of berries. This statement was perfectly true, and the wretched man was fleeing from the avenger.

August 23rd, Iron Creek.—This beautiful stream derives its name from a strange formation, said to be pure iron. The piece weighs 300 lbs. It is so soft you can cut it with a knife. It rings like steel when struck with a piece of iron. Tradition says that it has lain out on the hill ever since the place was first visited by Na-ne-boo-sho after the flood had retired. For ages the tribes of Blackfeet and Crees have gathered their clans to pay homage to this wonderful manitoo. Three years ago, one of our people put the idol in his cart and brought it to Victoria. This roused the ire of the conjurors. They declared that sickness, war, and decrease of buffalo would follow the sacrilege. Thanks to a kind Providence, these soothsayers have been confounded, for last summer thousands of wild cattle grazed upon the sacred plain.

————

BATTLE RIVER, *August 23rd.*

The future inhabitants of these rich lands will find no lack of water power. This river, which rises in the pine forest near the foot of the mountains, and runs parallel with the Saskatchewan for more than 400 miles, is from its source to its confluence one continuous water power. The same may be said of the numerous tributaries of the larger rivers. All supply water at an elevation that will meet any demands for milling purposes.

26*th.*—Hard times. All order has fled. Men, women, and children are seen running in every direction in search of berries, roots,—anything that will satisfy the craving of hunger. For days they have had scarcely any food, and the great camp which so recently passed over this trail felt nothing for us; but how true, "Man's extremity is God's opportunity." Earnestly have we prayed for help, and now it comes. One of our hunters signals from a hill that buffalo are in sight. Hurrah! Hurrah! In a moment all the sufferings of the past are forgotten. The runner mounts his horse and dashes off in the direction indicated. From a rising ground we witness the charge. In less than ten minutes ten fat beeves are on the ground. Exclamations of joy are shouted by the women. These buffalo will be baked, boiled, and roasted for supper.

September 1st.—The great camps, the Edmonton, the Victoria, and the Blackfeet, numbering more than 10,000 souls, are all within a short ride of each other.   The plain Crees, driven in by the Blackfeet, have fled to us for protection.   The Edmonton people have had a skirmish with the enemy, and blood was shed.   Last evening the Blackfeet sent us word that they would fight us to-day at noon, and 300 men are anxiously waiting for them.   I have ventured to say they will not come.   A long experience amongst red men has satisfied me that when they threaten they seldom strike.

The Blackfeet are also aware that there are two missionaries in the camp, and their superstition will prevent them from coming.   With feelings not easily expressed, I sat upon a knoll and reflected upon surrounding circumstances.   Our tents are pitched upon one of the most magnificent plains in America.   Unnumbered herds of cattle are fattened on free pasturage.

Hundreds of lakes offer drink to man and beast.   Here we have a perfect realization of a hunter's dream, and what are the facts ? sin has poisoned all.   In these camps we see the untrained development of the vilest passions, hating and being hated.   There is no peace for the wretched people. Their degradation cannot be written.   One hardly knows how to apologise for the mis-statements of intelligent tourists, who have travelled these plains.   They must have written as they ran.   Their descriptions of the noble, virtuous, honest native, are all from the pure ideal point of view.

Let them come down to real work, and study the language and life of the people, and live amongst them, as your missionaries have to do, and they will be able to appreciate the wonderful change wrought on many of them by the teaching of the Gospel. Delivered from the slavery of demon worship, the Indian is the happiest of men. Once truly converted to God, he presents a noble specimen of what the Gospel can effect. While under the influence of heathenism, his mind is filled with a strange mysterious dread. His religion teaches that an evil "Genius," that never slumbers, follows him from the cradle to the grave. Omens, presaging sorrow, are daily presented to his dark imagination. A significant word from a conjurer, the flight of a bird, or a dream, are all interpreted to foretoken death or sickness.

The pagan believes that his "Genius" instructs him in the hours of sleep, and the consequence is frequently awful. A Plain Cree, with whom I am acquainted, dreamed that his Puh-wah-gun, demanded three human victims, and he actually murdered three of his own tribe. A young heathen, whose father lives at our mission, fancied that his demon demanded three human sacrifices, and last summer he shot a young half-breed, with whom he was on the most friendly terms. A short time ago I conversed with this young man. He frankly acknowledged his determination to complete the number, alleging as a reason, that if he was not faithful to the instructions given, a fearful retribution would follow.

But I must stop, for were it necessary I could unveil some of the mysteries of paganism, and tell of deeds of darkness that would make the heart sick. War, murder, gambling, polygamy, and demon-worship are all producing their natural effects; and if civil law and Gospel light are not speedily brought to the rescue of these tribes, they will perish from the earth.

Making plain provisions in the hunters' camp, with all

its wild surroundings, the man of leisure may pass his time
very pleasantly; but there is another class, who find more of
fact than fiction in killing wild cattle—to this party belongs
the missionary.

A long winter stares him in the face.   There is no market
where he can go to for supplies.   Offer a man gold for flour
in the Saskatchewan and he would laugh at you. $60
per barrel has been tendered to the Hudson Bay Company,
and the money has been refused ; and no wonder, for every
pound of the precious luxury has been dragged over the 1,800
miles from St. Paul, and that in Red River carts.   But the
good time is coming.   The royal standard is now supplant-
ing the bunting of the Hudson Bay Company.   Brother
Dominionites ! our majestic rivers invite your steamboats ;
our natural road extending from the Winnipeg to the
Rocky Mountains, wide as the limitless prairie, is waiting
for your land transport.   This wild, uncouth younger brother of the confederation family only waits the chance for
development, and the youth will become, what geographically and naturally he really is, the heart and soul of the
country.   But I must go back to the camp, and the first
thing is to kill the animal, cut it up, and bring the meat to
your tent.   Then the process of curing and drying takes place.
Then follows pounding and making up pemmican.   True,
you can have help, but my experience of buffalo eaters goes
to prove that however numerous the servants, the master is
the greater vassal.   Then you must shoe your own horse,
mend carts, and what is more trying, keep a day and night
guard upon your animals, for horses are constantly disappearing very mysteriously.   These are some of the toils of
the hunter.   The missionary has additional ones.   Night
and morning he collects the people for prayer ; he must

visit the sick; his tent must be a refuge for the aged and for the afflicted. The avenger of blood is awaiting his time; the missionary must be the mediator.

Not long since one of our young men, influenced by jealousy, shot at his companion, but providentially missed him. The next morning I saw the offended man cleaning up his six-shooter, and he confessed to me, that he was watching his chance. In the evening, by the help of some friends, we brought the two together, and effected a lasting peace. Then there are the Sabbath services; these are highly appreciated by our people.

In some suitable place the Union Jack is hoisted on a pole; a crier goes round the camp, and invites all to unite in the worship of the one true God, and often have we felt while addressing the Stonies, the Crees, and the half-breeds,

"That labor is rest, and pain is sweet,
If Thou, my God, art here."

GEO. McDOUGALL.

Immediately after we find in the same manuscript the following, which in the light of events subsequently happening, is significant. Father had been brought into contact with Roman Catholicism and Roman Catholic priests; and, indeed, with many of the latter he had been on very friendly and neighborly terms, and yet, here is what he says. This would be the latter part of the year 1869:

The Papacy, the man of sin, is powerfully represented in this country. There are five priests to one Protestant missionary. They are anti-British in their national sympathies, and if we may judge the tree by its fruit, anti-Christ in their teachings.

Their converts have a zeal, but their fervor prompts them to propagate a system and not a Saviour. By them the Sabbath is desecrated, polygamy tolerated and the Bible ignored. Their churches are the toy shops where the poor heathen get their playthings, such as idols, beads and charms, and where the Anglo is denounced as no better than a brute beast; or to quote from one of their sermons, " No better than the buffalo that herd upon the plain."

They carry with them large pictures, representing two roads—one terminating in Paradise, the other in the bottomless pit. On the downward track all Protestants are travelling surrounded by demon spirits; while on the other road, throng all Roman Catholics, priests, nuns, etc.

By these baptismal regenerationists the sacred ordinance has been so desecrated that many of the heathen receive it as they would a charm from one of their sorcerers. One of the tricks played by these gentlemen is, when a child is born in a Protestant family, a female agent enters the tent, fondles the infant and then professing to show it to their friends, carries it to the priest, who baptizes the babe; but the policy of the missionary has been to avoid all controversy, and simply preach Christ. The very opposite has been the practice of the priest, and if trouble should arise between the tribes of this country and the whites, the cause in a large degree, will be at the door of the Papacy. These priests are hard workers, summer and winter they follow the camps, suffering great privations. They are indefatigable in their efforts to make converts, and these converts when made, if stripped of the external badges of Papacy, are still heathen; for of them it may be truly said, they have not so much as heard of a Holy Ghost. These poor baptized pagans have never been pointed to the Lamb of God.

Another letter to Dr. Wood about this time reads thus:

VICTORIA MISSION.

Many thanks for your timely advice in the *Missionary Notices*. Only let the Government act up to those suggestions, and untold trouble will be averted. We are doing all in our power to save the country from bloodshed. A large number of Crees and mixed bloods have signed an address to the new Governor, asking for a peaceable settlement.

Our position at the present time is one of the most perplexing possible. The Blackfeet are the trouble. They profess to be friendly with your missionaries, and yet kill our people and rob your missionaries. When good old Mas-kee-pe-ton was murdered, I felt it was time to take a stand. Since then they have made a raid upon Victoria, and some fighting has taken place. I then sent the Blackfeet a message, stating that I had often saved their lives and buried their dead, and that now they must send back the stolen property, and give me a promise never again to attack our mission. There reply was, "You harbor our enemies, and we must fight them." Since that time my son has ventured amongst them, and he intends going again in February. But I feel there is danger. These men have shed so much American blood, that there is no trusting them until they get a humbling.

Until a treaty is made with the Crees, it is highly important that my son John should be among the Plain Crees.

His thorough knowledge of the Cree language has been of great service to us during the past summer.

If our poor Indians are to be saved from the terrible fate of the American tribes, the earnest missionary must be the agency. Impressed with these feelings, I shall keep my son amongst the Plain Crees until I hear from you. He is there now, and I assure you our anxieties are not lessened by knowing that two murders have been committed on the track he was to travel, and these within the last two months. No change can be for the worse in this blood-stained land.

Next spring I expect to have to move my family into the woods until the men return from Red River and the plains, as there will be no safety along the banks of the river. Our plan is, what few men will remain in the country will reside at the mission, but the women and children we shall have to hide.

Fortunate for us the Blackfeet are greatly afraid of the Wood Indians. Pray for us. We are resolved, come what may, to remain at our posts. Woodville Mission is out of the way, and the Blackfeet dread the Stoneys. Brother Steinhauer is comparatively safe, being twenty miles from the plains. Last summer we had no crops, and flesh must be our food for many months to come. Since early fall I have suffered from inflammation of the eyes; this, with other trials, has often made my proud heart groan; but I trust my God will, according to the riches in Christ Jesus, uphold his unworthy servant. Knowing the deep interest you have felt in the poor Blackfeet, I will offer my opinion.

These men will yet be humbled by the Americans, and that very soon; things cannot rest as they are now; let us be ready to improve the first opportunity.

Their country is the finest part of the North-West, and must be occupied ; and it is worthy of note that twice in the last two years the buffalo have left the country. This will bring them to terms faster than military power.

On the plains the buffalo are the sole dependence of the Indian. In the meantime we must watch and pray. As regards the Cree, national interest, humanity, and love for perishing souls combine to make their case a pressing one. Had we ten faithful laborers they could all be well employed. At present there is a chance of a peaceful settlement with them. But I must close. I can, with difficulty, see the letters.

GEORGE McDOUGALL.

The following, which we have also discovered among his old papers, and evidently written about the same time as the preceding, will show his foresight, as also evidence his philanthropy and patriotism. The article begins thus:

"THE IMPORTANCE OF AN IMMEDIATE SETTLEMENT WITH THE PLAIN TRIBES."—Every resident in this country knows that a feeling of dissatisfaction prevails to an alarming extent among these Indians. Six years ago the sight of a pale face in a Cree camp was a cause of rejoicing; now the very opposite is the fact. One of the principal reasons is the rapid decrease of the buffalo. In the winter of 1867-8 these Indians suffered great destitution, and the whole cause is attributed to the whites. Recent events have added much to their previous dissatisfaction. In all past time they have regarded the honorable Company as the highest

representatives of the Queen.   Now a rumor reaches them
that a power greater than that Company will soon be here
to treat with them for their lands.   Injudicious parties
have informed them that their old neighbors have received
a large sum for these lands, and the Indian is not so ignorant but to enquire to whom has he ever ceded his hunting-
grounds.   They have no idea of civil government.   We have
spent days in trying to explain to them that they would be
justly dealt with, and the answer invariably has been : " The
Hudson Bay Company told our grandfathers that always,
and you missionaries have been repeating the same story for
twenty years, and yet nothing has been done."   These men
are exceedingly jealous of the miner and the settler, and a
collision with either party will bring upon this noble country all the horrors of not simply war, but massacre.

We have observed in the papers that much is expected
from the Hudson Bay Company's influence in settling with
the natives, and as regards the Wood Indians there is no
doubt but their assistance would be considerable ; but from
these we have nothing to fear, and as for the Plain tribes,
they have neither the power nor the influence to control
them.   For years their traders have not ventured into the
Blackfeet camp.

The last time they attempted a trade with these nobles,
their carts were robbed.   Some of the Plain Crees are very
little better.   Twice last summer they pillaged the Company's agents.   Of these Indians I speak from personal
observation.   For years I have visited them in their camps.

Last summer, in company with my son, who has a perfect knowledge of their language, we spent eighteen weeks
amongst them, attended their councils and listened to their
speeches, and the impression received was, if Canada is

going to extend her humane policy to these Indians, there is no time to be lost. At present there are agents that might be powerfully employed to effect a permanent settlement. West of Carlton there cannot be less than 700 mixed bloods. These are all anxious for civil protection, and a treaty with the Indians. The Hudson Bay Company's servants, who at present live by the sufferance of the natives, would gladly lend their influence.

Another party from whom we would expect much, is the natives that have been trained at the Protestant missions. Many of these are sufficiently enlightened to know the power of the white man, and on the whole are for peace.

Then there is still a lingering love for the Union Jack. Many of the Crees call themselves "King George's men," and they all dread American encroachment. With all the ardor of a Canadian who loves his country, and who desires for its honor that justice may be done this remnant of a once numerous people, I would advise that no time be lost in meeting them at their councils, treating with them for their lands, and by potent explanation, allaying the present excitement.

Let it not be forgotten that in the upper Saskatchewan there are at least 20,000 natives who by a wise and just policy can be made the friends of the Government. Let this once be accomplished and the country will speedily be settled. Between the Bow River and the North Saskatchewan there are gold fields of sufficient extent to fill this country with an enterprising population. There are now scores of families who would gladly settle in the neighborhood of Victoria, but the best friends of the country must discourage immigration until the Indians are treated with.

G. M. McDOUGALL.

The foregoing extracts from father's journal will fully show his views on these matters, but if there were mutterings of discontent on the Saskatchewan, when the packet arrived it brought tidings to the isolated settlements in the west of an outbreak in the eastern portion of the North-West.

The half-breeds and natives of Red River were said to be in rebellion. The months that intervened between this news, and the final suppression of the rebellion by the advent of General Wolseley and his command, were times of serious anxiety to us in the Saskatchewan. Father felt the responsibility keenly. There was a consciousness that the same influences which created disorder in Red River were working for the same purpose in the Saskatchewan. From Victoria constant communication was kept up with the Sweet Grass, the Big Bear, and the Wood Cree camps, the object being to counteract, if possible, any disturbing or disloyal influence. In the spring father became so anxious, not only in regard to the possibility of trouble, but also in regard to supplies for these missions during the coming year, that he determined to go to Red River himself, and was there during a short period of the reign of the rebels. He reconnoitred Fort Garry himself, and offered to be one of twenty men to surprise and recapture it from the rebels;

11

but if there were nineteen such men as himself in that country at that time, they were not to be found. Previous to his starting for Red River there had come up from the plains south of us rumors to the effect that the small-pox was among the Blackfeet and Bloods. Father had told us that if the disease reached this country before his return, to do all we could to scatter the Indians. His last words were, as he started for Red River : " Now, John, if the small-pox reaches the Saskatchewan, isolate the people as much as you can." Sure enough, the season had not far advanced, when we heard that the small-pox was among the Plain Crees. All felt then that it must inevitably reach us. Such was the lawless state of the country, such was the migratory habit of the Indians, that soon from camp to camp, and from post to post, the fearful epidemic was carried.

When it reached Victoria how we longed for father to return. There was no one in the country in whose medical knowledge we had so much confidence. As the Indians began to arrive, we did as father had instructed us, and urged them to separate and isolate themselves. Our words to them were, "If you continue in large camps, and congregate together, this disease will grow in power, will assume a virulent form, and will be almost sure death to any who may take it; but

if you scatter as you have been advised, very many of
you will escape the infection, and even those who may
have already become infected, may reasonably expect
the milder forms of the disease, if they do as we say."
This advice very many took, and there was a scatter-
ing through the wood lands and prairies of the north.
But in this we were thwarted by the directly contrary
advice of the priests.   They gathered the people together, they assembled them in meetings, and they
used our action in the matter as an argument against
us.   They said, " You now see who are your friends; as
soon as calamity comes, the Protestant missionary
drives you from him, while we say come to us;" the
consequences were that many of the Indians and half-
breeds gathered together, and died like rotten sheep.

At Victoria we closed the church, and dismissed
the schools, held no meetings, told the people as much
as possible to refrain from visiting each other.   " By all
means, as you love your families and your people,
keep away from the infection."   It was impossible for
us to do this with the poor ignorant Indians from
the plains, as they came around us in all stages of the
disease.   The writer was one of the first in the mission party to catch it.   But in the meantime many
had died.   In almost every fence corner around the
mission, all along the banks of the river, were the

dead and the dying.   In the midst of it, to our great
delight, father arrived.   The rebellion was over, but a
worse thing had come upon us.   No one can describe
the misery and wretchedness of such a time as this.
Night and day the missionaries and their families were
busy with the dying and the dead.

Letter from father at this time to Rev. Dr. Wood :

VICTORIA, *August* 16*th*, 1870.

Surrounded by circumstances that cannot be described, I
sit down to pen you a few lines.   The evening we left Red
River I learned that the small-pox had reached the Saskatchewan.   Anxious to be with our people we crossed the
plains in nineteen days, and at Carlton we met the destroyer
of the poor red man.   One hundred had died at Fort Pitt,
and along the road we encountered bands flying from the
plague, yet carrying death with them.

On reaching Victoria I found my worst fears more than
realized.   My son had induced the Crees to scatter, but
many, already struck down with the small-pox, were incap-
able of helping themselves.   Two days after my arrival
John was taken very ill, and is now in a critical state.   For
weeks my dear boy has had very little rest.   Day and night
he has waited on the sick and the dying.   Many of our best
members have passed away.   On Saturday, our most beloved local preacher, Thomas Woolsey, died in great peace.
His death has made a great impression.   Some of his last
utterances showed a depth of spiritual knowledge truly
astonishing.   Forgetful of his great sufferings, he spent his
last night on earth in exhortation, prayer and praise.

Glory to God, who, in the midst of Popery and paganism, proclaims His sovereign power to save to the uttermost.

At this mission, the past summer has been a time of danger and great anxiety. The Blackfeet, driven to desperation by the awful scourge which has cut off more then one-half of their tribe, have sought to propitiate their deities by murder and robbery. They have stolen our horses and killed our cattle; articles of clothing and human hair, infected with the small-pox, have been left in our village; and so reckless of life were these wretched men, that of a war-party numbering eleven, who made a raid on Victoria, ten died. Some of their bodies were found by our people. Sad new has reached us from the Mountain Stonies. The Blackfeet left clothing in their neighborhood; the thoughtless Stonies took the blankets, little thinking that one-half of their nation would be the price.

From Bro. Campbell I have not heard since my return. With White Fish Lake we have no intercourse. The last report was that the disease had not reached that neighborhood. What gives the greatest trouble in this land of robes and leather, is to find clothes for those who have recovered. We cannot allow them to return to their families with their infected clothing to spread the disease. Very little meets the wants of the poor Indian. Friends of suffering humanity, pray for us. Verily the judgments of a just God are now upon this land of blood and idolatry; and yet, of how many of these suffering creatures, it may be truly said "they know not their right hand from their left."

G. M. McDOUGALL.

Towards autumn there came a deceitful lull in the disease, and it became imperative to prepare for win-

ter.   Father's instructions to his son were, gather the
people together who are as yet disinfected and go with
them on to the plains.   In the first place, do all you
can to keep your camp from infection; in the second
place, do all you can to obtain provisions for the coming winter.   Accordingly we got ready.   As carefully
as possible we avoided the infection.   Sad was the
party under these circumstances.   There seemed to be
a consciousness that in this life we should not all meet
again, and so it was.   Our party had not been more
than two weeks away when the disease broke out in
the mission.   All were taken down with it except
mother.   Three of the household died in terrible agony,
and father recovering from the disease, and slowly re-
gaining his strength, with the assistance of my brother
David, themselves buried their dead.   Here are some
more of father's letters:

VICTORIA, *Oct.* 21*st*, 1870.

As there will be no other chance for writing until winter
expires, I send this on to Carlton, hoping it may reach you.

Since I last wrote, the harrowing scenes we have passed
through cannot be detailed.   Small-pox has swept away
hundreds.   To relieve the sufferers, and to seek to lighten
the sorrows of the bereaved, has been our work.   Of all men,
the ignorant, destitute red-man is the most wretched when
a strange disease appears amongst them; many have died
alone and unattended.

Not a few have sought relief by plunging into the river, and multitudes who recovered from the disease have perished from destitution.

We have sought by every means in our power to stop the spread of this great destroyer, and with deep gratitude I record the fact, that, up to the present date, not one of the old settlers of White Fish Lake or Victoria have died of small-pox. Our trouble has been with the poor Plain Crees who fled to the mission in their distress. Many of these have died within sight of our door, and yet my own family, which, including adopted children numbers nineteen souls, have hitherto escaped. To God alone be all the praise.

Never was the arrogance and bigotry of Popery more manifest. Having taught their deluded followers to look to them as to a god, when the scourge first appeared they collected their people into large camps : the bodies of the dead, the infected, and the well, were all collected in the church. The spiritual power of the priest proclaimed the grand specific, but all has failed. At their mission, ten miles from Edmonton, upwards of one hundred have died, mostly French half-breeds, while numbers of the same people have died on the plains.

My son has gone with the Victoria camp to the plains. Our people must have provisions. Brother Steinhauer is out with his people. I enclose you a note written the day he started. Brother Campbell was here last week ; my son and he have arranged (D.V.) to start on a visit to the Mountain Stonies the first snow. Our poor Stonies! I fear most of them are gone. So great has been the mortality amongst these western tribes in the last eight years, that, but for the assurance that numbers have died in the triumph of our faith, our work would be most discouraging.

I have just received a letter from Mr. Hardisty, of Fort Edmonton. Two hundred of the St. Albert people are reported dead. There will be great distress this winter, the fall hunt being a failure. When I left for Red River I had three good horses, I took two with me, leaving one with Mrs. McDougall. The Blackfeet, during a thunder-storm, stole the horse from the door yard, and also killed one of our cows ; but these are small matters compared to the loss some have sustained. My most intelligent neighbors believe that Jesuitism is at the bottom of all our Blackfeet troubles. One thing we do know, that we have been represented to them as harboring their enemies, killing their people, etc. If ever the rights and liberties of British subjects are enjoyed by Saskatchewanites, the world shall know some of the dark deeds of the past two years.

Geo. McDougall.

Victoria Mission, December 2nd, 1870.

When I wrote you last our people, accompanied by my son, were starting for the plains. We used every precaution to prevent all that were infected with small-pox from going with the party. I followed them to their first encampment, and there we detected small-pox, and had the family removed. Thanks to the Great Preserver of life, no other case occurred among them during their long sojourn. This was the more remarkable, as they passed over a part of the country where the Blackfeet had left scores of their dead in an unburied state. At one place they passed the tent of the celebrated chief Nah-doos, the principal murderer of our Mas-ke-pe-toon.

An enemy more to be dreaded than the Cree had overtaken him ; and now, surrounded by numbers of his dead warriors, his body was left to be devoured by wolves.   From a pole projecting at the top of the tent floated a Union Jack, and the warrior's coat mounted with ermine.   We have not yet ascertained the number of Blackfeet who have died with small-pox ; but judging by the number of unburied bodies left at each encampment, the mortality must have been very great.   In the Upper Saskatchewan, not including the Blackfeet, there cannot have been less than one thousand deaths at the French half breed settlement ; near Edmonton, three hundred have died, and many are still afflicted.   Our position at Victoria has been a trying one.   The more intelligent of our people, who acted upon our advice given them in the early part of the season, have escaped the disease.   There has been but one case here among the English half-breeds ; and our old chief, who, with a part of his band fled to the woods on the breaking out of the disease, has, up to this date escaped the sickness. Yet great have been the sufferings we have witnessed.   Our mission has been a centre to which the diseased from all parts came destitute of food ; and, in dread of the Blackfeet, they crowded around the mission house.

We have had to bury the dead and wait upon the dying. In these labors we have been assisted by the Hudson Bay Company's officers, who at the risk of their lives, have never failed at the post of duty.

EXTRACTS FROM JOURNAL.

September 25th, 1870.

The disease first appeared in my own family, and on the 13th of October our youngest daughter, aged eleven years, died. How precious to our bleeding hearts her dying words! Flora loved the Saviour.

October 23rd, 1870.

We are now passing through deep waters, all prostrate with the fearful disease, except Mrs. McDougall, and she exhausted with watching. Yesterday I felt it was high time to set my house in order. For two nights my mind has been wandering, and what course the disease may take I cannot tell; but I bless God, come what will, I feel all is right. I feel I am an unworthy sinner, but a sinner saved by grace. I had a long conversation with my much-beloved daughter, Georgiana, and gave her directions as regards the future. Little did I think, as she stood beside me the picture of health and youthful energy, that before I fully recovered myself, I should lay her in the grave.

Last night she was taken very ill, and to-day it was distressing to witness the change that has taken place in her appearance.

24*th.*—Last night I resolved to sit up, and not allow myself to sleep. Most earnestly I prayed that I might retain my senses, and, blessed be God, He has heard my prayer; and to-day, though the disease has developed, I am enabled to wait upon others.

25*th.*—This morning a Cree woman came to me and begged that I would baptize her infant grandchild, who had been taken ill with the small-pox. I walked to the tent and attended the duty, and though the day was stormy, I have felt no evil consequences.

26*th.*—This morning I heard a person crying at the garden gate, and on going out found a worthy Cree, whose family were all suffering from the sickness. The poor fellow said that his only son had just died in his arms, and he wanted me to help to bury him.   I went and dug the grave, and assisted the afflicted father in burying his child. In less than a week he himself was in his grave.

28th.—This morning I buried our Anna.   My son-in-law, Mr. Hardisty, dug her grave at the foot of Flora's. They were warm friends in life, and in death they have been but a few days parted.   Anna was fourteen years old. She was the daughter of the late O-ga-mah-wah-shis.   He gave her to us a few hours before his happy death.   She was the best looking native girl in this part of the country; of a docile, tractable disposition.   We were all much attached to Anna.

November 1st, 1870.

At five o'clock this afternoon our Georgiana breathed her last.   The last intelligible words she uttered were prayer. A few days before she was taken ill she told her sister that during one of the services in the church her soul was greatly blessed, and we all observed a marked change in her conduct.   The great Master was evidently preparing her for a better life.   Georgiana died at her post.   For months she has labored incessantly for the good of this suffering people.   Conversant with their language and modes of thought, she proved herself a judicious counsellor.   My kind neighbors, Messrs. Hardisty and Tait, brought the coffin and placed it at the gate, and my son and self carried her mortal remains to the grave.   When we were filling in the earth, he uttered an expression which found an echo in my poor heart, " Father, I find it hard to bury our own dead ;" but just then the words of the apostle were applied with such force to my mind that I could not restrain myself from shouting them aloud: " O, death, where is thy sting ?

O, grave, where is thy victory? Thanks be to God who giveth us the victory through our Lord Jesus Christ."

November 13th.—This morning I returned from my sixth visit to a miner who lives about ten miles north of Victoria. The poor fellow has been very ill with inflammation of the lungs, and I trust the Lord is sanctifying his affliction. About twelve o'clock last night I noticed that he was very much excited, and, throwing up his hands, he exclaimed, "O, wretched man that I am! The son of a pious mother, often have I laid these hands upon her knee and repeated prayer, and many a time she has led me by the hand to the class-meeting—and yet, for twenty years, I have forsaken my mother's counsel. Oh, my God, I will return!" And my afflicted neighbor has returned, and found peace in believing. And here let me say, take courage, ye praying mothers. This is the third case I have met with among these wild adventurers who, in the time of extremity, have turned their thoughts to their pious mothers. The mother may never know it, but a covenant-keeping God has answered her prayers.

November 18th, Quarterly Meeting.—After an intermission of two months, we have again ventured to hold a public service. Our meeting was deeply affecting: there were vacant seats to remind us of the past. There could be little done in the way of preaching. Both missionaries and people wept before the Lord. I could not refrain from reviewing the past. Since my connection with the mission more than one hundred adults, natives, have passed away. Some of these were marked men and women, earnest Christians, who were a credit to the Church of Christ. Then the multitude of dear children, my own among the number, who delighted in singing the sweet songs of Zion.

These have all disappeared from among the living. At first
sight there was something very discouraging, and we felt
that if in this life only we had hope, we should be most
miserable, but ours is a work for eternity, and these are not
lost to us. Our love-feast was a season of power; the Com-
forter was present.

November 22nd.—Started for Edmonton in company
with Captain Butler and Messrs. Hardisty and Clarke.
The Captain is out on a tour of inspection, and takes a
deep interest in the great North-West. He declares the fact
is humiliating to an Englisman that so fine a country should
have been totally neglected. The weather is very fine,
the plains free from snows, stock of all kinds taking care of
themselves. When I told the Captain that the average of
such was two out of three, he appeared surprised, and declared the country superior to parts of the United States
immediately south of us. At Fort Edmonton we were
cordially received by Mr. Christie, whose long residence in
this country enabled him to give much valuable information
to the Commissioner.

On Monday I was present at a novel ceremony (at least
in the Saskatchewan), the swearing in of Mr. Christie and
Mr. Hardisty as magistrates for the western territory.
Their power will be nominal until troops are sent in; and
yet it will enable us to protect ourselves against the whiskey
traders, for if we cannot enforce the law here, we shall
assuredly follow them to Manitoba. We have also the
prospect of a monthly mail next summer, and this will be a
grand advance when compared with one express in the year.
While at Fort Edmonton, through the kind co-operation of
Mr. Christie, we raised $100 towards finishing the Stoney
church. I would add that I have recently heard from all

the brethren in the District.   They and their families have,
up to this date, escaped the pestilence.

Geo. McDougall.

The writer will never forget the experiences of a
day in the beginning of the winter of 1871 and 1872.
With the blessings of heaven, we had loaded our carts,
succeeded in keeping the infection out of our camp,
though several times we had to stand with our guns
in our hands to do so.   We were on our way home,
and about forty miles from the mission, when we met
an Indian, who told us the sad news : "Three have
died in your house before I left, and it was said your
father was not expected to live."   Mounting a horse,
the writer started for the mission.   Some time after
dark, he walked up to the gate of the yard.   Hearing
a step on the plank walk, from the gate to the house,
he presently heard a voice say, " Is that you, my son ? "
"Yes, father," was the answer. "Don't come in," was the
response ; "all are doing as well as can be expected in
the house.   Your sisters lie yonder ; they died happy.
Go out to your camp ; keep those who are free from
the infection from it, as much as you can.   Good-bye,
my son."   And the heroic, unselfish missionary turned,
though he himself tottered, to another night's vigil.
Cold weather set in and helped to break the disease ;

but weeks elapsed before it was possible to raise the *quarantine*, and meet once more.

After all, our settlement, and the Indians who really belonged to us, and who listened in spite of other influences, suffered very, very much less than any others throughout the whole country. East and west and south, all over the land, the death roll was fearful; fully fifty per cent. of the people being carried away. A large portion of these lay unburied. During all this time there was not a single medical man nearer than Fort Garry. A story got abroad among the Plain Crees that it was the missionary at Victoria that brought in the small-pox. The more intelligent Indians knew that it was the Plain Crees themselves who had brought the epidemic up from the south, where they had gone on one of their horse-stealing expeditions; but with the dissatisfied and now desperate and ignorant class, any story, laying the blame on some one upon whom they could vent their vengeance, would be received gladly. The winter of 1871 and 1872 was, in consequence of this, a time of serious anxiety. Here we will insert the following, written to Dr. Wood:

VICTORIA, *March 1st*, 1871.

The medical gentleman sent up by the Board of Health is now returning to Red River, giving us an extra oppor-

tunity for communicating with the frontier world. There
have been very few cases of small-pox since the doctor's
arrival. Whether the disease has exhausted itself, or
whether it will break out afresh in the spring, are questions
anxiously asked by many. That the whole country is
infected there is no doubt, and it is beyond the powers of
man to disinfect an Indian community. Our hope is, that
the disease being so violent last summer, and in most com-
munities very few escaped the contagion, we may now be
relieved from its further ravages.

Our consolation is, we are in the hands of a God who
will order all things right. As regards the business of the
country, we are placed in a difficult position ; according to
the Governor's proclamation, nothing in the shape of trade
can be exported. The Hudson Bay Company, in order to
meet the wants of the poor Indians, have, at much sacri-
fice, continued their business. To withhold from the
natives ammunition and clothing would have been death
to them. What the merchant will do with the pelts taken
in return for these things is now a question. Notwithstanding all adverse circumstances, our work is progressing
encouragingly.

February 5th.—Chief Factor William J. Christie spent
the Sabbath at Victoria, visited our Sabbath-school, and
in a very feeling manner, addressed the scholars. Next
morning, as Mr. Christie and Mr. Hardisty were about to
start for Lac la Biche, a letter was handed me from the
former, which, upon opening, I found to be one of condo-
lence, and also expressions of deep interest in, and kind
sympathy for, the cause of missions. Enclosed were two
fifty dollar cheques, one for the White Fish Lake School,
and one for Victoria. This liberal donation was most

gratefully received, for the appropriation made by the Board, though ample for other lands, will scarcely cover the board bill of a teacher in the Saskatchewan.

Thursday, 9th —Accompanied by my son, I met Mr. Christie and the Company's officers at White Fish Lake. The school examination, which occupied the whole day, was most satisfactory ; the exercises were commenced by Brother Steinhauer presenting a very appropriate address to the Chief Factor ; then the young Crees were called upon to perform their part.   Their attainments in reading, writing and spelling, geography, arithmetic and Bible history, were very creditable, so much so, that the gentlemen present expressed themselves as agreeably surprised at the proficiency manifested by these native children.

Great credit is due to Mr. Ira Snyder, their teacher. Our pious young brother labors hard for the spiritual good, as well as the mental improvement, of his large school. Our young brother is also a useful local preacher, rapidly acquiring a knowledge of the native tongue ; and, if faithful to the grace bestowed, will at some future day, occupy a still more important position.   At the conclusion of the exercises, Mr. Christie addressed the parents and the scholars. He commenced by referring to a circumstance connected with his own family.   Nine years ago his youngest daughter passed the winter at Norway House ; there she had for a companion the youngest daughter of the missionary ; from her she learned to sing many of the sweet pieces which he had listened to that day.   When the first epidemic passed over the Saskatchewan, his dear little daughter was one of the sufferers.   Among her last utterances were portions of those hymns.   This fall his mind was deeply affected when he heard that the little maid, from whom she

12

had learned to sing, had fallen a victim to the small-pox.
He could only say to the afflicted parents, " Let us console
ourselves with the happy assurance that our dear children
are now where no sorrow will mingle with their songs."

My son was requested to take note of the address ; and
in the evening, to the great satisfaction of all present, he
repeated it, almost verbatim, in the native language.

Brother Steinhauer deserves the sympathy of the
Christian Church. His people are decidedly in advance of
all other natives in the Saskatchewan. Principally by his
own labor, he has built a good parsonage. On the ground
floor there are five commodious rooms ; the partitions, the
panel doors, the neatly ceiled walls, all display taste and
workmanship. Assisted by his people, he is now collecting
material for the building of a larger church. If some of
our liberal friends would lend him a hand by assisting to
procure nails, glass, etc., they would be investing in what is
a paying enterprise. A church in which the blessed Gospel
is preached will be a greater power for subduing and con-
trolling these Plain tribes than stone forts, rifle or cannon.

Saturday, 11*th*.—We returned to Victoria. The inter-
ruption which our school suffered during the time of pestilence retarded its progress, but now we are doing well, and,
notwithstanding the great scarcity of provisions, the average attendance is from forty to fifty. Over twenty of these
can read the Word of God, and almost the entire school understand English. We have also a week-night reading
class. Our plan is a very simple one, but it has proved a
great success. Some six or eight are called upon to read
pieces each evening. They are allowed to select their own
reading, with the understanding that nothing immoral or
fictitious will be introduced. So far we have had to admire

the good taste displayed.   Great effort has been made to acquire a thorough knowledge of the reading, and the different tastes have given us quite a variety. Christian biography, temperance, history, and dialogues all pass before us.   In fact, so profitable have been the exercises, that we intend to introduce them among the natives, training those who understand the syllabic characters to interest their people with portions of the Bible.   Notwithstanding that famine and pestilence have swept over us, our poor people have not been unmindful of their obligation to do something for the support of the cause of God.   Last fall we intended to hold missionary meetings at each appointment, but were prevented by the epidemic.   For local purposes we have received the following sums: For White Fish Lake School, $250; for Victoria School, $100; from Chief Factor Christie, Esq., $100 for general school purposes; and from our friends at Edmonton, to assist in finishing the church at Woodville, $100.   In addition to this they, last summer, presented Brother Campbell with two horses, our good missionary being so unfortunate as to have lost all his horses the winter previous.   1 regret that my son, who left here fifteen days ago for the great camp at Elk River, has not returned, for important information relative to the work among the Plain Crees might have been given.   John had a three-fold commission: he carried out with him the Government proclamations, which we are all anxious should be explained to that people; he was also commissioned to convey to the chiefs tokens of good will from the company, and presents in tobacco and ammunition.   His journey will be a hard one, for the camp is more than half-way to the boundary line.   The buffalo having left the Saskatchewan, the Indians have had to follow them on to the bare plains, and we fully expect to hear of great suffering, if not death, from starvation.

GEORGE McDOUGALL.

To add to the general misfortune, the buffalo kept far out on the plains. The Indians stuck to the last points of woods and were barely existing. In the month of February they began to break across a seventy-mile stretch of bare plain to the Hand Hills. Here they obtained wood and were so much nearer to the buffalo. In the meanwhile they kept away from the Hudson Bay posts. They began to counsel among themselves, and presently word was brought in to Edmonton that the Indians were gathering for a war of extermination among the whites. They laid the blame of all their calamity upon these. The Chief Factor of the Hudson Bay Company, then in charge of the whole district, felt anxious. He travelled down to Victoria and conferred with father, and the result was that father sent his son, equipped by the Hudson Bay Company, to visit these Indians, and to ascertain the true state of affairs and, if possible, to clear away the misapprehensions that were on their minds, and to negotiate with them in the interests of peace.

No one will imagine for a moment that the father's heart was not full of the strongest earthly affection for his boy, but such was the character of the man, he would not hesitate for a moment in such a case. As parent and as superior in authority, his words were, " Go and do your duty." The three weeks it took to accomplish this work, in a country where there were no means of communication, were weeks of anxiety, not only in the mission house at Victoria, but all along the river. The mission was a success. The clouds were dispelled, and the heart of many a native was made to feel that the good Great Spirit was yet his friend, and that He was mightier than all the powers of evil.

As spring came on, the buffalo took a northerly turn as they moved eastward, and helped to smooth matters, by furnishing meat for these travelling camps.

April 1st, 1871.

Now that the dark cloud, which for more than a year has enveloped this land, begins to disperse, we naturally enquire, For what reason has God, in His mysterious providence, suffered these terrible things to come upon us ?

More than one-third of the inhabitants have been swept away by that fearful disorder, the small-pox, and yet, however paradoxical the statement, the language of Joseph is applicable : " But God meant it for good to bring to pass as it is at this day, to save much people."

In the last three or four years, the Plain tribes have manifested a ferocity among themselves, and a contempt for the white-faced stranger, very striking when compared with their past history; so much so that all hopes of a peaceful settlement seemed to vanish.

Last summer the Master of Life permitted a visitation which has deeply humbled these vain men; and while we witnessed with anguish of soul their indescribable sufferings, we also felt it was better to fall into the hands of God than into the hands of man; better far to perish by pestilence than by sword—the inevitable end if no change had come. We have good reason to believe that their afflictions have been sanctified.

My son, who has lately returned from visiting the Plain Crees, reports them as very quiet, and anxious to listen to the missionary. Quite a number have resolved to give up the chase and settle at our missions.

The poor Blackfeet, who for months, and that on Dominion soil, have been pillaged and depopulated by American alcohol traders, are now sending us messages of peace. Their case on the part of our Government demands immediate attention, not only for the sake of the unfortunate natives, but also as regards the peace and prosperity of this great country. If multitudes of unprincipled men, to avoid the laws of their own country, can at pleasure cross our lines and establish scores of low grog-shops, then from the Missouri will roll back on us such a flood of intemperance and demoralization as shall make the fairest part of this North-West one vast field of blood and contention.

In the upper Saskatchewan we are face to face with a powerful and enterprising neighbor, who, with astonishing energy, is erecting military and trading posts; and this would give us no anxiety if similar improvements were made on our side. The American punishes with severity the infringement of the law prohibiting the sale of intoxicating drinks to Indians, but Benton and Montana traders cross the 49th parallel, and, in defiance of the law, carry on their loathsome traffic. To quote from a letter of a close observer, who spent December and January among the whiskey vendors of Belly River : " No language can describe these drunken orgies ; more than sixty Blackfeet have been murdered ; and if there can be a transcript of hell upon earth, it is here exhibited."

I know there are those who will say, " All right, the sooner the red-skin is swept from the plains the better." Thank God this is not the voice of Canada ; her sons and daughters have been trained to sympathize with the poor Indian, and view with commiseration his struggle for existence before the ever-increasing flood of civilization.

In the Saskatchewan they must be protected, and the only way by which this can be done is to establish a military post at Bow River, where the revenue laws would be enforced, and impartial justice to red and white administered. The present time is favorable for a settlement with these tribes. An enemy more terrible than war has, to some extent, subdued their fighting spirit. Their country is the finest part of the North-West. I have travelled in every part of the western prairies from Lake Winnipeg to the mountains, and I have seen nothing to compare to Bow River section. Gold, coal, and timber abundant; numberless small rivers and rivulets flowing from the mountains, with their snow-capped peaks, add to the prospect a sublimity and beauty that cannot be described. Statesmen of Canada, here is a field worthy of your noblest efforts ; Christian philanthropists, to you we appeal on behalf of a trodden down and rapidly perishing people ; the precious gift they need, you can bestow. The Gospel is not an experiment. Scores of Stonies and Crees have proved its power to save to the uttermost, and they are now in heaven.

Last fall, when the terrible pestilence was upon us, I saw the poor Cree lying upon the cold earth, in the last stage of the loathsome disease ; the long night passed without drink, fire, or clothing, yet within that heaving bosom lived a power no human misery could crush—the deathless love of Christ.

Our ardent desire is to proclaim this matchless love to every man, woman and child in the Saskatchewan. Alas ! we have not the power. Our numbers are too few. I am now entreating the Mission Board for one additional man— ten could be well employed. Citizens of favored Canada ! to you and to your children are given the hunting-grounds of the poor Indian. Their natural day will be short; hasten to their rescue, remember them in your prayers, forget them not in your alms-giving, and He who has purchased them with His own blood will reward you.

I shall not attempt to narrate the wonderful events of the past year. Notwithstanding the consolations of religion, our hearts are sad ; many of those for whom we have labored for years are gone. Not less than 140 Stonies are cut off, our poor Crees broken, scattered, and strewn like the leaves of autumn. Aged native Christians and sweet little Sabbath-school songsters all gone ! All that is mortal of two of our own dear daughters lie in the mission garden ; we mourn, but not as those " who have no hope, for if we be- lieve that Jesus died and rose again, even so them also that sleep in Jesus will God bring with Him." We will try and be grateful for mercies. In the midst of death all our mis- sionaries have been spared. Twice the restraining power of God was very manifest in the preservation of my own family. Once Mrs. McDougall, my eldest son, and two daughters were in the field, weeding turnips, and, not a hundred yards from them, secreted in the long grass, lay eleven Blackfeet. They came to pillage and murder; but, as they afterwards acknowledged, were restrained from firing. At another time they crawled through the barley, so as to witness all that was doing in the house, but did no harm. My son and a Christian Cree were crossing the river in a skiff, and as they were in the act of hauling the boat up the bank, a ball passed between them, tearing up the earth close to their feet.

Many are the hair-breadth escapes experienced by members of this mission, but no blood has been shed. Surely the good Lord has prevented it ! In the past winter we have been trying to redeem the time ; our services both on Sabbath and week days are well attended, and some of the heathen are receiving the truth.

The day-school is faithfully taught, and a more orderly class of children could not be found. The Sabbath-school averages between fifty and sixty. Twenty of these are committing the Wesleyan catechism to memory, and some of them have completed the task, and have also correctly recited the fifty-two lessons in Scriptural doctrine. With a thorough knowledge of this admirable system of theology, we have no fear that any of our young people will ever become Papists. Monday evening is spent in public reading and singing.

A course of lectures has been delivered on " History," by Hudson Bay officers and others, calculated to prepare our people for the change now taking place in their country.

Temperance has been prominently kept before their

minds, and, with few exceptions, both young and old have pledged abstinence from all that can intoxicate.

On Sabbath afternoon we preach at a small settlement ten miles distant, and there a promising Sabbath-school has been established, where both European and native, who once blasphemed, now spend a part of the holy day in teaching others to read the Word of God. Next to the spiritual interests of our people, we have felt it our duty to labor for temporal improvement. In this we are greatly encouraged. More seed will be sown, and more land culti- vated this spring than in any previous year. With the powerful aid of the Hudson Bay Company, material has been collected for a flour mill.

Thankful for past mercies, hopeful for the future, with sincere hearts, we would give to God the glory for all the good that has been accomplished.

GEO. M. McDOUGALL.

CHAPTER VII.

Moves to Edmonton—Three Years' residence at this place—Journeyings and experiences connected with this new field.

IN the spring of 1871, father began a mission at Edmonton. For a long time Edmonton had stood on the list of stations in connection with the Methodist Church. This simply meant that it was, in a way, the headquarters of the evangelist missionaries, Rundle and Woolsey, who had been the guests, when at home, of the Hudson Bay Company. As yet no mission had been attempted, but as Edmonton was the head of the district, and the mercantile depot for the whole country, and was on every hand beginning to attract settlement, it was thought by the District Meeting that this post should be taken up, and the chairman himself was the best man to do it. Accordingly father moved up to Edmonton and began work. This season the streams were very high, and in one of the many situate between Victoria and Edmonton, father came very near losing his life. Descriptive of this, we will insert right here a leaf or two from mother's journal :

June, 1871.

We moved from Victoria ; my husband and self, and two of our neighbors, started on our journey to Edmonton. The roads were very bad, the banks of every stream we came to flooded. The two first were crossed without very great difficulty ; the third, called Sucker Creek, was raging, the waters rushing and foaming with swiftest speed. When I first saw it, I wondered how we were to cross it, and turning round to speak to Mr. McDougall, I saw he was preparing to cross by moving the luggage from the buckboard and placing it on the cart ; and when ready he drove down the bank of the stream, and at the same time spoke to the boy who was driving the cart to follow. Scarcely had the horse struck the current when he was thrown on his side, and horse and buckboard, with Mr. McDougall standing on the buckboard seat, were carried down the river. There were trees projecting from the bank into the stream on either side, and presently all were carried under one of these trees, and horse, buckboard and driver were tangled up together by the force of the current. This was repeated several times, and very soon all disappeared around the point out of my sight. All this happened, as it seemed to me, in a moment.

I tried to speak, but could not. I turned to the men, but I saw them running through the bushes down along the bank of the river, and my first thought was to follow, and I was going to do so, when the boy with the cart drew my attention.

He had been directed to follow, and had just got down the bank of the stream, and the horse had stopped, with the water above the shafts, and I went to see if I could do anything to help him.

I found that it was impossible, the steep bank shoving
the horse and cart towards the current. We could not possibly back the cart out. I told the boy to sit still, and I
spoke a few words to the noble animal, and he stood perfectly quiet, bracing against the current as if he knew both
life and property were at stake. In the meanwhile I was
continually looking to God, and praying that my dear husband's life might be saved from a watery grave, and while
doing so, I realized all would be well. I had only to wait,
but the time seemed very long before anyone came, and
how my heart leaped for joy when I heard his voice, calling
to me, and I ran to meet him.

His first words were, Let us praise the Lord for the preservation of my life. He had been near the gates of death.
The wet and sticky reins had become wound around his
arm, and thus sometimes under the buckboard, and sometimes coming to the surface, he had been dragged along with
the horse and rig ; and not until he had succeeded in biting
away the reins from his arm was he able to swim for the
shore. He said the horse had struck a bar at the foot of a
steep bank on the other side of the river, and was standing
there with just his head and neck out of the water. He
said, if I can get across now with this other horse, I may
yet save him.

He stopped not to change his wet garments, but took off
his boots and plunged into the water, and unharnessed the
horse which was in the cart, and mounting him, he struck
out into the stream. This horse was a strong, spirited animal, and soon I saw Mr. McDougall and his steed climb
the other bank, and, disappearing down through the woods,
presently he came back with the other animal, and both
horses and master looked as if they were ready and fresh

for any other emergencies that might happen. In talking over this circumstance the same evening with old Harry House, one of the neighbors who accompanied us, he said : "Mr. McDougall and the animals' lives were saved in answer to prayer. Madame," said he, "you must call to mind the prayer that was offered by Mr. McDougall this very morning before we started on our way. Near the close of his prayer he asked God to bless us in our journey, and asked Him that the lives of both men and animals entrusted to them might be precious in His sight, and it was so." Tears of joy were streaming down the good old man's cheeks as he thus spoke to me of the day's experience.

Friends rallied round him, and in a little more than a year he had comfortable mission premises, and better than this, a flourishing cause. In the meanwhile he visited the missions under his charge, White Fish Lake, Victoria, and Woodville. The amount of work in the building of a mission in a new country, one thousand miles from a saw-mill; in erecting mission-house and church, and establishing school can be estimated only by those who have gone through the experience.

In the spring of 1873 he started for the southwestern country, and reached the Bow. The reader will remember that all the region southwest of Edmonton was for hundreds of miles the Blackfeet country. Here the Blackfeet, the Sarcee, the Piegan, and the Blood were allied against the Stoney and the Cree. This was the scene of many a tragedy. In this

fair land and on the banks of the Elk, in the valley of
the Bow, along the margins of High River and Old
Man's River, and in the intervening countries, many a
white man had come to a terrible end. To make
matters worse, an illegitimate traffic was being smuggled in by a wild class of lawless men from the
southern border. The southwestern portion of our
country was at this time the rendezvous of the hard
cases. From Fort Benton and other parts of Montana
alcohol was being smuggled across the line, and whiskey, warranted to craze and kill, was being manufactured at different points. Very little was known about
this region by the people who lived in the north
country. Very few white men, though they resided in
the Saskatchewan for years, knew anything of the
Bow River country.

Hundreds of Indians along the North Saskatchewan, notwithstanding their migratory habits, have
never been so far south, but the mountain Stoney,
whom the missionary met on previous trips, and also
at Woodville and the old mountain fort, said it was a
goodly land, and importuned for a mission somewhere
in that region along the eastern base of the Rocky
Mountains. These Mountain Stonies were our people.
They had been faithful to us, and they had won
father's heart, and his sympathies were with them.

Though few in number, they had held their own, in the whole width of British territory along the eastern base of the mountains. They had done this against the combined hosts of the plain tribes. Father admired their pluck ; moreover, his foresight told him that by planting a mission somewhere at the foot of the Rocky Mountains in that southern region, with these Mountain Stonies, with their warlike prestige, as its body-guard, not only the interests of Christianity, but the peace of the country and the future settlement of it, would be in a large measure secured without collision with the natives.

Subsequent events have more than verified his prophetic action. To explore for this he, in company with a single native, travelled through this region. Reaching the Bow, they came out upon this valley a few miles east of the present Morley. It was about the end of May or first of June. I can imagine father, as he sat upon the hill, picturing to himself the changes that he felt were coming. Little did he then dream that in front of him and at his feet would, in less than fifteen years, lie the steels that belt the continent. Little did he think that up this valley would roll the tide of the world's westward travel ; that down the slopes before him would pour the produce of China and Japan ; and yet he knew it was coming.

Having seen the country for himself, he came back and endorsed the Mountain Stoney's opinion of his native land. He, in company with other missionaries, the same summer, travelled across the plains to Winnipeg, and met at this place Drs. Punshon and Wood, also John Macdonald and other friends, who had come up from the east to shake hands and encourage the missionaries. A delightful missionary conference was held; the hearts of the so often isolated missionaries were cheered by conference with these eloquent and wise brethren.

Father secured the endorsation of his scheme for the opening of the new mission at the foot of the mountains, which he had so much at heart, and then bidding the brethren good-bye, he, with others, again set their faces westward. It was his privilege to travel across the plains in company with Sandford Fleming, the chief engineer of our Government, and Dr. Grant, now Principal of Queen's College, Kingston, and Professor Macoun, the famous botanist; they, in turn, were fortunate in falling in with the old pioneer missionary. The following spring, early in the month of April, he and his son visited the Mountain Stonies, who were then camped in the valley of the Bow, at the foot of the Rockies, continued the exploration of the country, and came to the conclusion that no

13

more central place for the new enterprise could be found than in the Bow Valley. While on this trip the missionaries remained several days with the Stonies, and travelled with them southward along the mountains, holding meetings morning and evening, in short, all the time, with these people.

At this time father assured these Indians that he would do all in his power for the planting of a mission in their country. Then retracing their way, the missionaries travelled homeward by a different route, keeping along the mountains, and then striking easterly towards Pigeon Lake, they came across another large camp of Indians, moving out from the woods to the north. Spending some time with these, they continued their journey and came to Woodville from the other side. Father then went on alone to Edmonton. The following letter to Dr. Wood is descriptive of this trip :

EDMONTON, *May 28th*, 1873.

According to previous arrangement, April 29th, I started for Bow River, and in the evening met my son at what is called the Forks of the Mountain Road.

May 1st.—At the foot of the Bear's Hill we fell in with a party of Victoria Crees, most of them our own people. With these we spent some time in religious exercises ; and, after exchanging prairie news, we pushed on to Battle River, where we met another party belonging to the same place. The head man of the camp is one of the noblest

specimens of a Christian native I have met with in this
country.   Our friend Noah invited us to his tent; we made
our supper on a yellow crane.   With these we held two
services and baptized two children, and were made acquainted with a fact demonstrating the power of Christianity on the native mind.   An aged, blind woman visited our
tent who, some months previous, had been cast away by
her inhuman children.   They had long felt the old woman
a burden, and one morning while she was asleep they all
slipped away from the camp, leaving her, as they expected,
to perish.   Our good brother and his party found the unfortunate mother, and were taking the best care of her in their
power.

On the evening of the second we reached the north bank
of Red Deer River.   For four days we had been travelling
through a country ready for the agriculturist; a rich black
loam resting upon a clay bottom; abundance of the finest
pasturage and the purest water.   Once across the Red
Deer River, and the traveller observes a change.   Here the
celebrated bunch grass begins, and the tough, level sod of
the northern prairie disappears, and the soil is so loose that
your horse sinks at every step, and wherever the badger
had thrown up the earth, we observed a mixture of lime-
stone, gravel and clay.

Springs and streams are abundant, and although the
climate has not been practically tested by the agriculturist,
there is not a doubt but that, for stock-raising purposes, it
is one of the finest countries on the continent.   In winter
there is scarcely any snow, and in summer the horse-fly and
mosquito, so numerous in Manitoba and the Saskatchewan,
are seldom seen south of the Red Deer.

Sabbath, 4th.—We spent at Dog Pound Creek, where

we enjoyed a magnificent view of the mountains. In the afternoon an old bull came down to the spring to drink, and not being disturbed, he fed beside our horses until the next morning.

Monday, 5th.—We travelled up the Little Red Deer, a beautiful river, the banks of which are well covered with aspen and pine. In the afternoon we killed a bull, and I caught a young calf, and we camped near to a large sulphur spring, where waggon loads of the mineral may be collected. It is also in this neighborhood where the natives find alum. I have seen them with specimens of it weighing from six to ten pounds.

On the afternoon of the 6th we struck the Stoney trail, and were a little discouraged to notice that they had passed some eight or ten days before our arrival. In the evening we camped on the bank of the Bow River, close in with the mountains. The prospect was one of the grandest I had ever witnessed, and Morleyville will yet become the favorite resort of the tourist.

Wearied with a hard day's ride, we selected a spot for our night's encampment where we could have a full view of the mountain sunset. Our camping equipage is very simple; we have no tent; a pair of blankets, a kettle and axe, a little flour, tea and sugar, and a piece of oil-cloth to protect us in time of storm, constitute our baggage.

There being no game laws in force, and having studied the nature of wild animals as well as wild men, with the blessing of Providence we have no fear of starvation. Just as we had settled down for the night a stranger made his appearance among the hills, and cautiously approached our camp. In this solitary lawless land a certain amount of suspicion marks the first meeting of all travellers; but here

was one of our own good Stonies ; he had seen our camp
smoke from afar, and made haste to inform us that his people had been waiting some nine days on the opposite side of
the river, hoping the missionary would pay them a visit.
We at once packed up and moved to the camp, where we
were received with a volley of fire arms, and a hearty shake
hands from young and old.

Here we found 42 tents, 73 men, 82 women, 58 boys, 71
girls, 199 horses, 24 colts, and 169 dogs.   A stranger
might smile at us in placing the dogs on the catalogue, but
the mountaineer knows how to make use of this kind of
stock.   The dog has to pack from 25 to 100 pounds.   I
saw some of them carrying an eight-skin tent, that is a tent
made of eight moose or buffalo hides.   We were at once
conducted to the Bear-paw's tent, where we made a good
supper on the flesh of a white swan ; then we all united in
singing a hymn in the Stoney language, and in thanksgiving to our common Benefactor.   But there was no sleep for
the weary ; the Stonies were so overjoyed at our arrival,
that prayer and praise were continued until morning.

On the morning of the 7th we moved out on to the plain
and had a general meeting, after which, in company with
the two principal chiefs, we started on a prospecting tour.
They had supplied us with a pair of first-class mountain
ponies, and the object of our ride was to visit some fish-
lakes that lie in the bosom of these mountains ; also to in-
spect the timber and hay grounds, etc.

Our mountaineers led us off at a good canter up hill and
along precipices, then descending into valleys where the
descent was almost perpendicular.   At first I felt a degree
of hesitancy in following these reckless fellows ; but seeing
that their horses carried them safely over ground where a

Canadian horse would have broken his neck, I whipped up, and for the remainder of the day kept alongside of our guides. In the afternoon we came to the great chasm in the mount through which the river rushes.

From a very high foot-hill we gazed on this prospect with admiration and wonder. Within three miles stood the grand old mountain, the wild goat and sheep sporting on its highest summit. At the foot of the hill, and in perfect ignorance of our presence, a band of buffalo were feeding on the richest pasture. To the right of us, and on the north bank of the river, lay the location which we have selected for our new mission.

In the rear of the plain there are large hills covered with valuable timber, and from these elevations scores of little streams run down into the valley. Further on, beyond the first range of mountains, there is a large lake which the old Indian tells us is bottomless, and the water so clear that salmon trout can be seen at a depth of thirty-five feet. In fact I was surprised at the clearness of these mountain lakes and streams. Late in the evening we returned to the camp tired and hungry.

At the evening service it was decided that on the morrow we should pitch southward, our people having an engagement to meet the Kootanies about the end of May. I had now ample opportunity for observing the conduct of this singular people. Twenty-five years ago they embraced Christianity, and though most of the old people have passed away, and they have only been occasionally visited by your missionaries, and for several years have been exposed to the destroying influence of whiskey-traders, yet, with few exceptions, they have been faithful to their religious principles. Many of them can read the Bible. In every tent there is family prayer ; they are passionately fond of singing. The week we spent with them was emphatically a camp-meeting. We retired to rest, listening to the voice of song, and awoke in the morning to hear the Stonies engaged in the same exercises. Sabbath, the 11th, was a day of incessant labor. We baptized thirty-one children, and married one couple, and at midnight lay down to rest, grateful to God for blessing the day. Monday, the 12th, at mid-day we left for the Saskatchewan, and crossed the High Water River; and on the 13th, with a great deal of difficulty, we succeeded in fording the Bow River. Expecting to meet some Stonies, we made a straight course through the country to Woodville, and on the evening of the 16th reached Battle Lake, where we found eighty of our people.

On Sabbath morning we preached to this camp, baptizing four children, and then rode over to Woodville, where we found two hundred waiting for us. In the evening we administered the Lord's Supper to about sixty communicants. On Tuesday, at noon, I reached Fort Edmonton, grateful to God for all His mercies. In the last twenty-two days we have passed through some dangers and difficulties, rapid and dangerous rivers have been rafted, localities have been visited where only a short time before human blood had been shed, where the American whiskey-trader and Blackfeet had met in deadly conflict. But through all our exposure the Lord has preserved us.

Six hundred and thirty-five Stonies have been visited, and upwards of one hundred Crees ; and, best of all, the presence of God has been strikingly manifested in our services. To His name we ascribe the praise.

G. M. McDougall.

The same season the Secretary of the Missionary Society, the Rev. Lachlan Taylor, visited these missions. Father met him at Fort Pitt and travelled with him to White Fish Lake; from there to Victoria, and on to Edmonton; out to Woodville, back again to Edmonton; from Edmonton, out on to the big plains to the large Cree camps; from the Cree camps to the mountains, being captured, and after two days released, by the Blackfeet *en route*; from the mountains in Bow River, south-eastward to Fort Benton, on the Missouri, taking in the famous Whoop-up country by the way. Then bidding the Secretary good-bye, and having delivered him within the possibilities of stage and telegraph lines, father returned for the most part by a new route across the country to Edmonton. Most of this travel being accomplished by him in the saddle. The greater part of the trip was subject to constant danger, father taking his turn on guard, and in everything sharing the burdens of this long journey.

During the winter of 1873 and 1874 he visited the missions on the Saskatchewan, and worked away at his own charge, which was growing in interest. Anyone looking up the reports of our Missionary Society will see what was done by this newly-begun mission during the years of 1871, 1872, and 1873, for the general cause, which is a good index of all other matters.   In the meanwhile the missions at the foot of the mountains were begun late in the year of 1873.

In the summer of 1874 father visited the new mission, and was very much encouraged with the results already achieved.   Made some journeys into the mountains during his stay, and then returning to Edmonton, began to make preparations to go to his native land, for which he had received a hearty invitation for himself and mother from the Missionary Committee of our Church.

The two following letters will describe the experiences of this time.

EDMONTON, *July* 20*th*, 1874.

Last Friday we received the first mail for six months.   I heartily thank you and our worthy President.   The only damper to the joy of Mrs. McDougall is—for she is very anxious to see her friends once more—that we cannot leave until a supply arrives.   I have spent too many hard days in the Saskatchewan to leave this mission until our men come. The last six months have been the hardest I have seen in the mission field.   Popery is rampant, and we have hard work to hold our own. After visiting Victoria, on April 1st, I went to Athabasca, where we have over thirty Stonies and other adherents, then to Bow River, and last week to Lake St. Ann's.   In making these journeys I have forded, rafted, or swam thirty rivers.   It is twenty-five years since the mountain streams have been so high.

I have now to take Woodville, and then, should help come, the long trail to Red River. For the first time I am nearly used up. John, subject to my consent, was appointed agent by the Government to visit the Blackfeet and Stonies, and explain to them the policy of the Government in sending troops, etc. All expenses to be paid, and $1,500 to be distributed in tea, tobacco, powder, ball and flour.

Believing the appointment to be providential, Mrs. Hardisty and I sent off a man to bring John in. He will have to report to the officer in charge of the troops. I shall request him to send you a copy. I have sent on to Red River a meteoric stone weighing 400 pounds, the great memento of the plains, and requested Brother Young to forward it to your address. I intended it for Victoria College, but shall be guided by your advice. Please have an eye if it turns up.

EDMONTON, *July 20th*, 1874.

Since the winter packet arrived we have been all in the dark as to matters civil and ecclesiastical, but fondly hoped that, during the summer, there will be a change for the better. Since the month of April I have made some laborious journeys; first to Victoria, then to Athabasca, and subsequently to Bow River. I felt it was a duty not only to our people, but also to the isolated mission family, to make a run to Morleyville.

Wednesday, June 5th.

Accompanied by Mrs. McDougall and one of my daughters, we left for the Mountain, and as the streams have been unusually high, we built a handy little punt, and mounted

it on a cart.   On a number of occasions we found the benefit of the arrangement, for the mountain streams were all
foaming.   The journey from Edmonton to Morleyville was
made in seven days, including the Sabbath, and only those
who live 200 miles from their nearest neighbor can realize
the pleasure with which we were received, not only by the
mission family, but also by a camp of Mountain Stonies,
who very fortunately arrived the same day.   In the evening I went with my son to visit an old patriarch, Kis-chee-
po-wat, a man who was once guide to Mr. Rundle, and who
was with the pioneer missionary when he ascended the
mountain now known to travellers as "Mount Rundle."
This venerable native was evidently, to use his own language, very near the great camping-ground ; but rich in the
consolations of the Gospel, and one of its blessed fruits was
very apparent in his case, for while the aged among the
heathen are often left to miserably perish, the family of this
old man treated him with the greatest kindness.

Sabbath was a day of special blessings, and in the love-
feast many were witnesses of the power of saving grace.   I
was much gratified with the efforts that have been made to
establish this mission.   Finding it impossible to build a
church sufficiently large to accommodate the numerous congregations, the missionary has run up a rough building,
covered it with bark, floored it with pine brush, lighted it
with parchment windows ; and here Blackfeet, Crees,
Stonies, and the traveller from other lands, meet to worship
the Lord of all.   In the meantime, timber has been prepared for respectable buildings ; sashes, nails, etc., brought
from Fort Benton, and we hope by next summer a fair start
will be made on this important mission.

Having a few days at command, I made up my mind to

prospect the adjacent country.   Our first excursion was up
the Bow River Pass.   The distance from Morleyville to the
foot of the mountains cannot be less than fifteen miles, the
most deceptive prospect I ever gazed upon, for the general impression is, when you first look across this beautiful
valley, that a ten-minutes' walk would take you to the base
of these snow-capped peaks, and yet we were two hours and
a half in reaching the entrance of the pass, at a smart
canter.   As we approached the great canyon, I was forcibly
impressed with the thought that there stood before us a fit
emblem of both time and eternity.   Of time, for the scene
was ever changing.   As the sun mounted higher in the
heavens, and the snow began to melt on the summits
of the mountains, small streams rushed over vast precipices
and spent themselves in spray before they reached the
foot of the mountains.   To the north of us, a heavy
thunderstorm enveloped the peaks, and we noticed, when
it had passed over, that at a certain elevation there had
been a heavy fall of snow.

In a few days' sojourn in these mountains the prospect is
ever changing.   Then there are the huge rocks, in some
places presenting a perpendicular wall 6,000 feet high,
grand representatives of the everlasting, and yet these shall
pass away.   While sojourning among these mountains, I
was profoundly impressed with my own ignorance.   Here
was a grand field for the geologist, and all I knew about
the science only increased curiosity.   Here is a perfect
paradise for the botanist, for among the multiplicity of
flowers and plants, I think I have seen some new specimens,
but find it difficult to classify.   And here I have seen the
wild goat upon the mountains, and my party have killed the
big horn sheep, the mountain marmot, and the large black

partridge; even the rabbit and the squirrel are unlike anything I have seen in other parts of the Dominion.   Here is
a grand field for the naturalist.

But, anxious to show the resources of our mission, we
resolved to visit Lake Taylor.   Marvellous stories had been
told us by the Stonies of this strange sheet of water; and,
after a careful inspection, we were certain the half was not
told us.   The lake is about eight miles long by one mile
and a half wide, and probably very deep, located between
two huge mountains, and evidently full of the finest trout,
for standing on the shore my party caught eight very fine
specimens.

The Stonies tell us they sometimes take them forty
pounds in weight.   In fact, every stream we met with was
full of salmon and brook trout.   This beautiful lake is not
more than twenty miles, in a straight line, from the mission.
While camped on the shore our Stoney guide pointed out a
path that led straight over the mountain to Morleyville, but
when requested the next day to take us by this route, he
replied, if it were the end of August, in place of June, he
would willingly do so, but at present the snow is too deep
for horses.

Such are the contrasts in this strange land.   Close by
our feet the strawberry is ripening, the gooseberry nearly
ready for use, and yet not half a mile distant the snow is
still several feet deep.   While conversing with my son, who
has just returned from Benton, I gathered a good deal of
very useful information in reference to the state of things
on our frontier.   The past winter has been one of unusual
activity on the part of the fur traders, and a large amount
of valuable furs have been carried out of our country.   I
observed in the *Notices*, that where I had stated in a letter

referring to their transactions one year ago, "that more than 50,000 robes had been carried out of British territory by these whiskey-traders," one cipher had been dropped by some of my cautious friends, making it "5,000." The secular papers that had copied the paragraph also made it "5,000."

Now I reiterate my statement, on the best authority, that more than 50,000 robes have been traded from our Indians annually for a number of years, and that nearly all the return that these wretched people have received at Benton, for what was worth $250,000, had been alcohol. And the terrible effect on the tribes is very apparent. Ten years ago the Blackfeet were rich in horses, and no observer could visit their camp without being struck with their fine physical appearance as a body of natives; now they are an impoverished, miserable-looking race. Last winter the usual amount of shooting took place; and the worst feature of this sad work is, the innocent suffer, and not the guilty. But as the Indian kills the first white man he meets for the death of his friend, no traveller is safe on these plains until a stop is put to the infamous conduct of traders.

While I was at Bow River our people found the body of a white man, who evidently had been killed by the Blackfeet; and since our return to Edmonton a report has reached us that a young man who was in the Hudson Bay Company's employ last winter had been killed on this side of Elk River. And all this catalogue of crime and death can now be traced to the unprincipled whiskey-trader. I have frequently received letters asking for information as to this country, and in which reference is made to the *Missionary Notices*. In answer to such parties, we would just say, as far as our observation goes, that one of the best stock-raising countries in the

Dominion will be found south of Elk River.   The horned cattle at our mission arrived at Morleyville late last fall. Most of the oxen had been worked through the summer, and those belonging to the missionary performed a large amount of labor in the winter ; and yet these cattle, although having to feed themselves, were fit for a trip to Benton early in the spring.   To those who may wish to settle on the eastern slope of the mountains, it may be useful to know that both provisions and stock can be bought much cheaper in Montana than in any part of the Dominion.   I saw two enterprising Canadians who, this spring, bought fifty head of four-year old oxen for twenty-four dollars each. They are bringing them over to the Saskatchewan, and I have been informed by my son that half-breed Texan cattle can be bought for even less than that ; and there is no doubt in my mind but that the day is not distant when, on our Dominion soil, we will be able to compete with our American neighbors in the stock department. As to cereals, I cannot speak confidently, for they have never been tried this side of Sun River.   One advantage we will have over Montana—we shall not have to irrigate, for up to the forty-ninth parallel there is, most seasons, an abundance of rain. As to the Indian question, which seems to deter many from making their home in this great country, I would just remark, that, should the Government give us protection, the best informed in the country are of the opinion there will be very little trouble with the Indians.

If they are judiciously treated by the Government, we apprehend no difficulty in settling the Indian question. Two things we would earnestly impress on the attention of those in authority in the country : First, that no notice be taken by the civil powers of the crimes that have taken place in the past.   If every murderer were to be arrested, there would be no end of trouble, and the Government would most probably become involved in civil war.   The next difficulty will be to know who are Dominion Indians, and who that cross our lines are not.   And this, I apprehend, will be a difficult matter to decide.

The Blackfeet proper have all along been regarded by the Americans as their Indians ; but from all we know of them, they can never be induced to settle on the American side.   The Piegans and Bloods receive annuities at the American agency, and yet they spend a large part of their time on our side, and frequently trade at the Hudson Bay Company's forts.   Now this is a question that will have to be settled before we can treat with these tribes, and until it is done we cannot expect to have peace on our borders.

Some of these remarks may appear foreign to the work of a missionary ; but our position is peculiar ; we are often importuned for information, and if anything we say can tend to the spiritual and temporal elevation of an unfortunate race, we shall feel amply rewarded.

CHAPTER VIII.

Visits Ontario—Pleads the cause of Missions—Takes a short trip
to the Mother Land—Once more sets his face Westward—Is
employed by Government to conciliate the excited Plain Tribes
—His tragic end.

ONCE more father drives across the plains. This
will be mother's first visit since she left,
fourteen years before. Those years have effected a
wondrous change in the northern part of the continent of America. A line of steamboats is on the Red
River.

The Northern Pacific crosses this river near the spot
where the missionary and his family fourteen years
before had camped ; at that time the whole country a
howling wilderness. No man appreciated better than
father did the possibilities of the great North-West,
and these wonderful changes which had already taken
place were sources of great joy to him.

Proceeding eastward, father reached Toronto in time
to be present at the first General Conference of our
Church in Canada. Here he met a hearty welcome, the whole Conference cheering as he entered its
presence. Some people may imagine that the invita-

14

tion to come home for a year, given by the committee
of our Church to the missionary in the far-off field, is
suggestive of a period of rest and recuperation, but
this is not so ; every energy of mind and soul must be
resurrected on the part of the returned missionary.
The tension of every nerve must be tightened a little
more, and the whole strain of wear and tear of such
a life as the southerly acclimated frontiersman is now
called to bear, proves often harder on him than the
rough years already passed through.

The crowded houses, the badly-ventilated and over-
heated audience-rooms, the cold and chill, though
stylishly arranged, sleeping places—all these things
affect his body ; while ever present to his mind is the
difficulty of presenting his thoughts to a different
people, and possibly expressing them in a language
to which he is not accustomed.   If there should come
a Sabbath in the course of the year, which the Missionary Secretary has not included in his programme
of work for the missionary, there are always a few
score of brethren who have been watching this opportunity, and by dint of importunity, they let the missionary off with two services and a Sabbath-school
address sandwiched in between.   And herewith we
would announce to all missionaries : If you want rest,
don't go home ; seek it elsewhere.   Father, during the

winter succeeding the first General Conference, pretty
well did the Eastern Provinces. Ontario, Quebec,
Nova Scotia, New Brunswick, were all visited in turn,
and everywhere the cause of missions and the great
North-West were his theme.

Towards spring he ran over to New York. Coming
back, he sailed for the Old Country. Addressed
meetings in London. Took a run into the Highlands,
from whence his forefathers had come, and then once
more turned his face westward.

He arrived in Ontario in time to be present at his
own Conference. Secured additional help for the work
on the Saskatchewan; and starting with mother and
his new mission party, he continued the journey westward, and to him, homeward; though in reality just
now he is without a home, for the missionary committee have concluded to undertake a new enterprise
and establish a mission yet further south in the region
of country which is known to-day as Southern Alberta.

Reaching Winnipeg by steam, the real work of the
journey now begins. Carts and oxen must now be
purchased. Transport provided for families Fortunately for the missionary and party, they meet at
this point with Mr. David McDougall, than whom
there is no better guide or frontier traveller on the
continent. He couldn't be much less, being the son of

his father. Just at this juncture news is brought
over the plains of trouble among the Indians and
half-breeds in the vicinity of Carlton, and westward
beyond it. The facts were, the Government was
proceeding with telegraph lines, and railway, and geological and other surveys. Material was being poured
into the country, and all this, prior to treaties with the
Indians. No explanations had been made, and no
wonder that the natives were concerned about these
things, which ought to be felt by any man of equitable
mind as something altogether " too previous." Surveys were stopped, and serious trouble was anticipated.
Father's opinion was sought; and he gave it as his
view that the trouble had arisen because of a lack of
understanding on the part of the Indians. That if
proper explanations had been made prior to these surveys having been attempted, he believed there would
have been no trouble. Immediately he was requested
by Lieutenant-Governor Morris, of Manitoba and the
North-West, to undertake this mission. Accordingly,
receiving his commission, he started with mother, and
proceeded directly to Carlton.

From Carlton he went to Prince Albert, and having
met the natives in these vicinities, he then started out
with his little party westward on to the big plains.
Travelling from camp to camp, he explained these

matters to the excited Indians, and assured them, as
his instructions were, that the following year commis-
sioners would be sent into the country to treat with
them.   He was received everywhere with confidence,
and his words were believed ; and the Indian mind all
over the country was set at rest for the time being.

Having travelled westward to Tail Creek on the
Elk River, and thence northward to Edmonton, and
from thence eastward to Victoria on the North Saskatchewan, thus covering the territory, and reaching
the people most interested in this matter, he then
started for the mountains and Morley, and the recently
located mission in the valley of the Bow, at which
place he arrived simultaneous with his party, which
he had separated from on the Red River some months
before, and which had been coming as directly as
possible in those days to this its destination.   How
joyous the meeting of these missionary parties.   Some
have been laboring in the country, others are just
returning from the east, some are new-comers ; all
are here for the same purpose, the taking-up of this
land in the name of the Lord Jesus Christ.   These
men and women are here to sow the seed of Christianity and civilization, to plant the standard of
empire, to uproot and destroy the savageism of
the native, to restrain the cupidity and selfish-

ness of the new comer. Truly theirs is a mighty
work, and only by the grace of God can they do it.
Winter is already here. What are the plans for the
future ? Listen to the leading spirit as he speaks to
his son, the resident missionary at Morley : "John,
myself and teacher will have to stay with you this
winter ; it's too late now to begin 150 miles further
south without a chip of preparation as yet having
been made. We are both willing workers ; we will
jump right in and help you to put up your church
and other buildings this winter, and then I want you
to come over with us next spring to Old Man's River,
and give us two or three months with your men and
teams." "All right," I said.

In the meanwhile father's restless spirit moved him
on, and within a few days we were on a trip of explo-·
ration south along the mountains, our object being to
hunt up the site of the proposed mission, and also
make ourselves acquainted with the best way of reaching this point. Between two and three weeks were
occupied on this journey, during which time several
large camps of Indians were reached, and the oppor-
tunities for preaching the Gospel were many. The
new Fort McLeod was also visited, and father was
kindly received by the mounted police, this place
being at that time their headquarters. Returning

from this journey, the fact that our large party required a fresh supply of provisions came up; and while some of us went out on to the plains for this, father proceeded with building operations and other work connected with the mission. Owing to very severe weather, and the distance the buffalo had gone into the plains, the hunting party failed this time, and were forced to go home in a state of starvation. Late in December he started on a missionary tour to the mouth of High River, where there were several trading establishments, and also quite a number of Indian camps. Early in the new year he returned to Morley, bringing word that the buffalo were now moving westward, and that this was now an opportune time for striking for meat, and as this was very much wanted by our party, arrangements were made to go out. Horses driven in, sleighs mended, and, at the last minute, the man we expected to go with us was not forthcoming. In vain we looked for another, and then father said, " I will go with you, for we must have meat." Our flour was getting low, and there were many mouths to fill. We started for the hunt, and procuring fire-wood by the way, pushed out on the plain.

On the third day we came to the buffalo. The condition of the prairie for running with upshod horses

was very bad. The weather was extremely cold. However, we secured some animals ; but Saturday morning
found us with about half loads, and the weather getting colder all the while. We saw that the buffalo were
slowly moving westward, we concluded to go back
with our teams to the first point of willows, where we
could get wood, and there spend the Sabbath, hoping
that the weather would moderate, and the buffalo
draw nearer. We spent a quiet Sabbath in our leather
lodge. Our party numbered five. An Indian and his
boy, about twelve years of age, had joined us to
obtain meat for themselves. Our party proper was
composed of father and his nephew, a lad he had
brought from Ontario on his last trip, and the writer.

Monday morning, from a hill alongside of our camp,
we could see buffalo. Father and I, taking four sleighs
with us, and a little wood on one of them, and two
loose horses for running, started out towards them.
The Indian and his son, with one sleigh, accompanied
us. We left my cousin to look after the camp and
watch the horses. The weather had moderated some,
but the prairie was still very bad for unshod horses.

Coming as near as we could without starting the
buffalo, father took charge of the horses and sleighs,
and I attempted to run, but so slippery was the prairie
with its patches of snow and ice everywhere, that the

sharper hoofed buffalo could get away from the unshod horse.

Changing horses three times, getting one tremendous fall, which shook me up pretty well all over, I eventually succeeded in killing six buffalo. The Indian had not been successful. We gave him one and began the work of skinning and cutting up the other five. It was now late in the afternoon. We had butchered and put on to the sleighs three of the buffalo. We were at the fourth. While I was working at this one, father said, "I think I will melt some snow, John, and boil the kettle, and we will have a cup of coffee." Taking the little bundle of wood we had brought with us from the sleigh, father soon had a fire built, and the kettle boiling. It was now becoming dark. The coffee made, father said, "Come along, my son, this will do you good after the shaking up you have had to-day." We had a few small cakes with us. Eating these, and sipping coffee and talking about our work, thus the night came on. I remember there was an odd cake ; father said, " John, you eat that, you have been working harder than I have to-day." The coffee drank, we went at the buffalo again. Just as we were finishing the fourth animal, we heard the Indian call, and answering him, he came to us with his sled loaded with the animal which had been given him. Altogether then we moved on to the fifth animal, and now, with the Indian's help, we soon had this one skinned and cut up and loaded on to the sleigh. This being done, I put my running pad on one of the loose horses, and gathering up the lariat attached to the halter, handed it to father, expecting him to ride. I then said to the Indian, " Go ahead, now, and I will drive my sleighs after you." He said, " I don't know the way; I am a Wood Indian, I am not so much accustomed to the plains as you are." I said, "I will tell you the way; you lead off with your horse and I will drive our four sleighs behind you, and if I see you going wrong, I will shout to you." The Indian did as I told him, and I strung out our sleighs behind him. We were about eight miles from camp, and I should judge it was about eight o'clock at night. There was some wind blowing and some snow drifting along the ground, but overhead the stars were clear, and the night was fine.

As I walked behind the last sleigh, father would ride beside me, or, dismounting, sometimes walk. We conversed about the future, we talked about the orphanage that he hoped to build and be instrumental in establishing at the new mission he was to move on to in the spring.

We came to the valley of the Nose Creek. Here there was a long incline to the creek. The Indian

started off on a run before his horse, and I cracked
my whip, and sent my horses after him. Father had
been walking when we came to the top of this hill,
and as the rest of us ran down the slope, we left him
some distance behind. We crossed the creek, and were
nicely strung out on the flat on the other side of it,
and as fast as we could were making our way to the
gently-rising hill near the summit of which our camp
was situate. I should judge we were about two miles
from camp, when father having mounted his horse,
came up at a gallop. Instead of stopping behind, he
rode up alongside. I said, " Father, are you going on ?"
" Yes," said he. "I think I will go and get supper
ready. That bright star there is right over our camp,
is it not ?" said he to me. I looked, and answered,
" Yes." It was impossible for me to think that he
could go astray. The landmarks were extremely good;
the night was not stormy. Away he rode into the
darkness. Little did I think that I had spoken to my
father for the last time in this world.

We went on to our camp until we were within two
hundred yards of it, being situate down in a little
valley. When I came in sight of the spot I saw no
light ; my heart misgave me. I rushed the horses up
to the tent, and shouted, " Father ; father. Moses ;
Moses." (This was the name of my cousin we had

left in the camp that morning.)   But no answer came.
I jumped into the lodge.   There was no fire.   I felt
around, and found the boy buried under the buffalo
robes, he evidently having become frightened as night
came on.   I shook him up.   Said I, " Moses, did father
come ?" He said, " No ; I have not seen him."   I jumped
out and grasped my rifle, which I had fastened on one of
the sleighs, and fired several shots in rapid succession.
I told the Indian to shoot off his old flint-lock, and he
did so repeatedly, putting in large charges of powder.
Then I said to myself, how foolish to get so excited.
If father has missed the camp, he will be in before I
can get these horses unharnessed ; or he has ridden
past to hunt up our horses we left here to-day ; and
with this thought I went to work and unharnessed the
horses, and disposed of them for the night.   But no
father came.   We did the best we could.

The next morning, with the first peep of day-light,
I found the horses, and was glad to see that the one
he had ridden was not with them, for I had thought,
that father might have been thrown, and hurt badly,
and if so, the horse would come to his partners.   He
was not there, and again I said to myself, it is now
daylight, and by the time I get these horses back to
camp father will be there ; but he didn't come.   The
Indian and myself scoured the country the whole day.

We did it systematically. The Indian was a first-class moose-hunter. I was no novice in such work. Evening came without a clue; then I said, father missed the camp last night, and passing on up to the ridge west of us, Morley would appear so near to him this morning, that he concluded to go right on to the mission. Some one will come out to meet us to-morrow. This was my theory; the Indian thought so too. Since Sunday the weather had been moderating.

Monday night, when father left us, it was comparatively fine. Tuesday was a beautiful winter's day. Tuesday at midnight the weather was still fine. Shortly after this the wind changed, and a most terrific northwest storm set in. It was impossible to move on the plains. Sheltered as we were in the valley, we had hard work to keep the fire going. We said, No one will start from Morley to-day. The storm continued all day, and a greater part of the following night.

Thursday morning, bright and early, we started for home. Getting my party fairly on the way, I left them to come on, and hurried home, reaching there late Thursday night, but father was not there. Then he must have gone to Calgary. We hurried down to Calgary. There were no tidings of him. We secured help and began the search. Saturday afternoon we found the horse.   Saturday night we heard from some half-breeds that they had seen a man leading a horse, the whole description corresponding to him and his horse.   The time they had seen him was on Tuesday afternoon.   Some continued the search, and others went for more help, and on Sunday we had all the available force we could get out on the search, but the weather became intensely cold, and Sunday night we had to fall back on Calgary for food ard wood

We then saw the necessity of better equipment, and we went home and gathered in all our available horses and sleighs, and starting out with all the men we could get, we camped on the spot, and continued the search.

The following Sunday I was riding up a cooley, had dismounted and tied my horse, so that I might more effectually search the clump of brush I found there.   Presently I heard some one shouting ; running out, and getting on to my horse and moving up the hill, I found it was the man next to me in the line of search.

Said he to me : " They are making signs to me over yonder."

Ah, thought I, father is alive.   I had not yet given him up.   When I reached the now rapidly congregating party, my poor broken down brother said, " Oh,

John, father is dead; they have found his frozen body." A half-breed, one who was not with us on the search, but was out hunting, had killed a buffalo, and going back to his camp, had taken his horse and sleigh and was making a bee line as much as possible to where his buffalo lay, and in so doing drove right on to father's lifeless body. He put him on the sleigh, and took him back to his camp, and sent us word. Soon we stood beside his lifeless form. A kind native woman had spread her shawl over it. I lifted the shawl, and as I saw the position in which he had frozen, I said, "Just like him; he was thoughtful of others, even at the last moment." As I looked at him, and beheld his features, I said, "Whatever may have happened to father, towards the last he was conscious, and feeling that death was upon him, he had picked a spot as level as he could, and laid himself out straight upon it, and crossing his hands, had thus prepared to die." His face was perfectly natural. There seemed to me to be the expression upon it of conscious satisfaction. Reverently we lifted him and laid him on the sleigh, and solemnly we started on that Sunday afternoon on our homeward journey.

The next day the party reached the mission. Fortunately we had as our mission teacher at this time a medical man, Doctor Verey. I asked him to examine the body, but to disturb it as little as possible. However, no clue as to what caused his death was discovered. My own theory is, that some disease affecting either his heart or brain, so acted upon him that for the time being he was unconscious of his surroundings; otherwise I cannot explain his being lost. We left him clothed as he had lived and walked last, in Western costume, thoroughly prepared for storm, as he knew well by long experience how to be. Thus he had taken his last walk, and strength failing, had laid him down and died.

It was a sorrowful company that bore his remains to the grave. With trembling utterance we laid him in it, in sure and certain hope of a glorious resurrection. His work is finished, but not forgotten, nor yet will it be. A faithful son, a true husband, a fond and righteous parent, a real patriot, a faithful missionary, such was father.

We here insert his last letters, written to the Hon. James Ferrier, Montreal.

> MORLEYVILLE, BOW RIVER,
> ROCKY MOUNTAINS, *December 17th*, 1875.

HON. JAMES FERRIER, Montreal :

DEAR SIR—If our young friends of Great St. James will just glance at the map, and follow their missionary in his wanderings since we parted on that delightful Sabbath

evening, I am persuaded they will need no apology for my
not having written sooner. The journey to Winnipeg is
an old story. There we parted with our mutual friend,
the venerable Dr. Wood, and, accompanied by brother Man-
ning and the school-teachers, struck out for the great North-
West. After travelling with the party for some days, I
left them as we approached Fort Ellice; and having a commission to visit the Crees and Stonies, I made all possible
haste to reach Fort Carleton.

Here you will observe we had to cross the South Saskatchewan, a river which was formerly a terror to the
travellers. More than once I had to make a canoe out of
buffalo rawhide, and ferry goods and carts across the rapid
stream; now there is a ferry-boat. After visiting the Indians of Carleton, and explaining to them the great Queen's
letter, I proceeded down the river sixty miles to the Prince
Albert Presbyterian Mission, where I also met the Indians
of that part of the country, and was treated with great
kindness by Mr. McKellar, the missionary. Here I had
the pleasure of taking a leading part in the opening services of a new church, and was forcibly struck with the
fact that our country is greatly indebted to the missionary
for its material development. When I passed through this
country eleven years ago all was wild and desolate; now
there are three churches in the settlement, and where the
prairie grass waved but a few years ago, there are now vast
fields of the finest wheat; the settlers expect to have 30,000
bushels. Most of these people are mixed bloods, but there
are quite a number of Indians who regard Prince Albert as
their home.

Having completed the work in that section of the country, in company with a gentleman of your city, Mr. Ellis,
15

the geologist, I started westward, following up the South Saskatchewan. Now, in your favored land of railroads and steamboats, it may appear but a very small matter to travel from Carleton to the Rocky Mountains, and the day will soon come when it will be but a small matter here; but to me it was a very serious one. The buckboard was our mode of conveyance, the tent our lodging-place. There is not a twig or a bush for hundreds of miles, owing to the Indians having followed the buffalo so far out into the big plain, and we were therefore obliged to spend weeks in a woodless country. Now just look at the effluence of the Elk or Red Deer River. Here I met with a deeply interesting people, the Plain Stoney; they had seventy leather wigwams.

These children of the prairie were greatly pleased when I told them what the Gospel had done for their brothers of the mountains. Now run your finger along the map in a westerly direction, and your eye will catch a place called Buffalo Lake; some call it Bull's Lake.

Here, by appointment, I met our missionary party, and also my son from Morleyville, and a large number of Christian Indians from Whitefish Lake and Victoria. My next journey was north, to old Fort Edmonton, thence east to Victoria. At every point I met with a most cordial reception from our Indian friends, who were all delighted to hear that the "Great Ogeemah" was going to treat with them for their lands.

From Victoria we proceeded straight to Morleyville, by Edmonton. Now, just look for old Bow Fort, or Bow River; six miles east of that stands your mission. Having spent three or four days amongst the Stonies, accompanied by my son, I started for Fort McLeod. You will observe that, running nearly parallel with the mountains, there is a vast range of hills called the Porcupine. To find a road through the great valley was one of the objects of our journey. We were guided by the Stoney interpreter, James Dixon, a very remarkable man, who for years has been the patriarch of his people. James, in a five days' journey, could point out every spot of interest ; now showing us the place where, more than twenty-five years ago, the venerable Rundle visited them, and baptized many of their people ; a little further on, and the location was pointed out to us as where his father was killed by the Blackfeet ; then again, from a hill, our friend pointed out the spot where a company of German emigrants, while crossing from Montana to the Saskatchewan, were murdered—not one left to tell the painful story.

This occurred seven years ago. How wonderful the change ! We can now preach the Gospel to those very people who, but a few years ago, sought the life of every traveller coming from the American side. Just examine the latest Canadian map, and see if you can find Playground River. Here is the place where we hope to establish our new mission.

This beautiful valley and river is named after the wonderful Nahneboshou, the Indian deity. The red man believes that while this great personage was on an inspecting tour, he was so delighted with the prospect presented at this place, that he rested, and amused himself by playing with some stones ; some of them were pointed out to us, and I should think they are quite as large as the mountain in the rear of your beautiful city. From the playground of the deity we could see the mountains of Montana, the great valley of the Belly River, and the boundless prairie away towards the rising sun, and thousands of buffalo grazing on the plains; in the rear of us, our guide pointed to the place where the Stoney hunts the wild goat, and the big horned sheep, the black tail, the white tail, and the graceful antelope. No wonder the poor Indian sighs when he tells you the story of the past; a great change is now rapidly passing over this paradise of the hunter; yonder stands Fort McLeod, at the mouth of the Playground River, the grand old Union Jack waving over that very spot where, only two years ago, I witnessed the sad effects of a drunken fight between the whiskey trader and the Blackfeet. Here we visited a large camp of Blackfeet, and informed them that we hoped soon to open a mission for their benefit. The head chief, who is quite an intelligent man, spoke of the future with anxious forebodings, and I think his statements were correct; let me illustrate his position by comparison. Just suppose that all supplies were cut off from Montreal; all factories closed because there was nothing to manufac_ ture; the markets forsaken, because there was nothing to sell; in addition to this neither building material nor fuel to be obtained; how sad would be the condition of the tens of thousands of your great city.

Now, the situation of these prairie tribes is exactly analogous to this state. For ages they have lived upon the buffalo; with its pelt they have made their wigwams, wrapped in the robe of the buffalo they feared not the cold, from the flesh of this ox they made their pemmican and dried meat, while they possessed his sinews they needed no stronger thread, from its ribs they manufactured sleighs.

I have seen hundreds of Blackfeet boys and girls sliding down these hills on this kind of toboggan. The manure of the buffalo is all the fuel they had—in a word, they were totally dependent on the buffalo.

Now, these unfortunate tribes behold with amazement the disappearance of these animals, upon which they have existed for ages. Unfortunate people! nothing but their abandonment of paganism and conversion to Christianity can save them. Well, let us now go back to Morleyville.. We shall go straight across the bare prairie. There is no fuel, but we shall carry a few small sticks for our first encampment, and hope on the second evening to reach the timber. Our journey was far from pleasant; at times the storm swept past us, and at night we had but very little fire to warm us.

November 6th.—We reached the encampment of our friend Dixon; there were 380 Stonies present. Next morning we held a service, and though the frozen grass was the best accommodation we could offer our hearers, yet, no sooner was the announcement made, than men, women and children gathered round us, and sang with great energy, " Salvation, oh ! the joyful sound." Here I counted over one hundred boys and girls who ought to be attending school, and who, I hope, will be, as soon as we can get a place erected sufficiently large to accommodate them. I must tell you now how I expect to pass the remainder of the winter. Since our arrival we have built a place of worship, and fitted up a room for each of the families. Fortunately, my school master is a good carpenter, and I am an old hand at building, so we have resolved to assist my son in completing the mission church. The only appropriation made for this important mission was $500 ; the improvements now in progress will cost considerably over $3,000.

We cannot ask the Society for another appropriation under existing circumstances; so, if the Lord gives us health, we intend to do the work ourselves. Perhaps my young friends may enquire, Why do you not hire somebody to do the work? The answer is simply this : In a country where the mounted police are paying mixed bloods $90 per month as guides and interpreters, and where a stock-raiser pays his herder $150 per month, it is not easy for missionaries to procure laborers. Some future day, when this great country is filled with Christian men and women, we shall be able to build churches just as you do in Montreal. At present, if your missionaries would succeed, they must not be afraid of a little manual labor. I expect next week to visit the mounted police on Bow River ; if spared to return, I have a number of Indian facts which I hope to send you.

Your affectionate friend and missionary,

G. McDougall.

————— .

MORLEYVILLE, BOW RIVER,

ROCKY MOUNTAINS, January 6th, 1876.

HON. JAMES FERRIER, Montreal :

DEAR SIR,—In the midst of much confusion and toil, I send you another paper for your model Sabbath-school. I wrote you a short time ago ; as to the matter or manner, I shall be thankful to receive any suggestions from you or the intelligent teachers of your school. There is something that strikes on all hearts in the spectacle of a great man's funeral. The hearse, the solemn march of the procession, are both very impressive ; and yet the subject of all this show may have been heedless of the great Salvation, and, if so, is now suffering the doom of a lost spirit. No feelings of this kind trouble the heart of the believer as he follows the young disciple of Jesus to the resting place of the body ; of these it can be truly said, "Blessed are the dead that die in the Lord."

Reflections like these often cross the mind of the Indian missionary as he looks for the last time upon all that is mortal of one of his Sabbath-school scholars. In the past twenty-five years I have assisted at the burial of hundreds of these little red children. The squirrel now gambols in the boughs of the trees that overhang their graves, and the partridge whistles in the long grass that floats over the solitary place ; but the incidents connected with their short pilgrimage cannot be forgotten. Little Ka-be-o-sense was about three years old when his parents, and his grandfather, Ke-che-da-da, were converted on the south shore of Lake Superior, about sixty miles west of Sault Ste. Marie ; and, at the first camp-meeting ever held in that country, on Sabbath afternoon, while the Rev. Peter Jones was conducting the communion service, the mighty power of God was so manifest that many were constrained to cry aloud. To use an Indian idiom, this was the hour when the relatives of Ka-be-o-sense first sighted the promised land. His mother, a very delicate young woman, but one susceptible of strong impression, there consecrated herself to Christ, and from that moment religion was to her, not only a new life, but a passion. Henceforth she talked to her little boy about the Saviour, just as she would about some very dear friend ; she taught him to sing ; she brought him regularly to class-meeting and Sabbath-school ; and what is most gratifying to a pious mother, she observed that with the first awakening of the mind, the blessed Spirit was influencing and moulding the heart.

How fortunate when parents and teachers understand

and sympathize with a sin-sick child who longs to love the Saviour! This forest boy was taught the simplest truths of religion, and shortly we had scriptural authority for believing that our little friend was happy in the emotions of joy and peace. When nearly six years old, little Ka-be-o-sense caught a very bad cold, which, in a few short weeks, terminated in consumption. I was in the Sabbath-school when a messenger from the cabin of Ke-che-da-da arrived, requesting that I should immediately visit the little sufferer. On arriving at his humble abode, I at once perceived that the struggle of life had nearly ended; the dear child received me with a smile, and pointing with his finger to a corner of the room, said, "Jesus has sent for me; the heavenly people are waiting for me." His mother informed me that for more than an hour he had been directing their attention to that part of the room, and telling them that the angels of the Great Mun-ee-doo had come for him. He then requested us to sing, and while the songs of the earth calmed and comforted the sorrowing friends, the redeemed and saved spirit of little Ka-be-o-sense passed away to the realms of rest. With deep emotion we thought of the marvellous change which had taken place in a few moments. Present to the natural eye, was the humble home of an Indian child, the weeping friends and the lifeless body, but the eye of faith beheld the ascending spirit, the rejoicing angels, and above all, the welcome received from the adorable One, who said, " Suffer little children to come unto me." Before parting with Ke-che-da-da's family, I will briefly relate a circumstance showing the ardent desire of a native Christian to read the word of God. I had noticed that the father of Ka-be-o-sense always brought his Bible to church, and followed the reading of the lessons with marked interest, and the circumstance excited my curiosity. I knew he was what we termed an inland Indian, and that no school teacher had ever penetrated the wilderness where he was born. Approaching him after service, I said, "You can read?" and his answer was, "Yes." "Who taught you the letters?" "I do not know them," was his reply. "Then tell me how you can read." Without any embarrassment he replied, "This is the way. I observe that when you pronounced any of our words that they were broken up into small parts. (I would here state that at this time we used Peter Jones' translation, in which, though he employs English orthography, all the words are divided into syllables. That Muneedoo is written Mun-ee-doo.) When the white man says "Indian," you write it "Uh-ne-she-nah-ba." When I went to my tent, I would take a hymn-book, and ask my wife to repeat one of the hymns she had learnt by heart, and I soon became acquainted with the form of all the syllables." Now, the simple fact flashed upon my mind, that this poor Indian, by intense and unremitting study, had mastered every syllable in his language. May not something of this kind have first suggested to the ingenious and indefatigable James Evans, the first idea of the syllabic character. When the light of Christianity first reached this young pagan, he was about eighteen years old, and the fire then kindled in his young heart was no transient flame. Very few in two short years have labored harder or accomplished more for the good of their people.

Often, since my lot has been cast amongst these wild, sensual tribes of the west, I have thought of zealous Ah-nee-me-ke, and felt constrained to plead with the God of missions that He would raise up and thrust out from amongst the Blackfeet young men like Ah-nee-me-ke, filled

with the Holy Ghost. My young friend was not what men
called gifted; unlike many of his countrymen, he was a
poor orator, and his gift of song was very limited ; yet,
wherever this young man went, a blessed influence followed,
and, until his health entirely broke down, he was incessantly at work for the Master.

I have heard him plead with the Sabbath-school children,
entreating them to give their hearts to Christ, until all
were in tears. I have seen him kneel beside a hardened old
conjurer who had bewitched his people with sorceries for
many years, until he trembled, and began to pray. The
secret of all this young man's power was his entire conse-
cration to God. I can now recall my feelings when assisted by this devout young man, for though we greatly
rejoiced in his success, we saw that he was rappidly slipping
away from us. It was in the spring of the year when he
was first confined to his humble bed. I daily spent an hour
with him, and invariably came away blessed in my own
soul by the conversation and experience of this dying Indian boy. The last time I called upon him his father was
sitting by his couch, the rest of the family being out in the
sugar bush.

Taking him by the hand, I enquired how he felt, and his
reply was, "You have just come in time, for I am dying."
Just at that time a Church of England minister entered
the room. I informed my friend we were about to have
prayer, and requested him to lead, which he readily did.
Kneeling beside my native brother, I took his hand in
mine, and, while the man of God was commending the
departing soul to the Saviour which redeemed it, the young
disciple fell asleep in Jesus. When we arose from our
knees I informed Wah-bun-noo-sa of what had taken place.

In this old man there was still a leaven of paganism, yet he fully believed in Christianity. He said that three things had caused him greatly to rejoice : 1st. That two ministers had been present when his son died. 2nd. That his dear boy was so happy in the prospect of death ; and lastly, that the Great Mun-ee-doo had called his son away at exactly twelve o'clock ; and what specially filled his heart with gratitude was, that the sky was perfectly clear, allowing the departed a glorious ascent to the home of the Great Spirit. We did not, at that time, try to instruct this poor man by informing him that his son had entered that land where there is day without night. I shall be glad, at some future time, to inform you about some of our living Sab-bath-school scholars, some who have been rescued from the deepest poverty and ignorance, and are now creditably fill-ing positions of responsibility.

With kindest regards, I remain your missionary,

G. McDougall.

Trusting that this simple detail of the life of my father may stimulate some hearts to a broader patri-otism, and brighter Christian life, is the earnest prayer of the writer.

Morley, 1888.

ROCKY MOUNTAINS, NEAR VIEW.

MANITOBA AND THE NORTH-WEST.

THE reader of the preceding chapters will have wandered, in imagination, with us over an immense region of country. First, we went down the valley of the Red and Nelson Rivers, to the shores of the Hudson Bay, then turning westward we climbed the slopes of the continent into the shades of the Rocky Mountains.

Traversing the big plains and woodlands, situated immediately to the east of these mountains, we camped southward on the banks of the Missouri, and went northward, on to the tributary streams of the great McKenzie, flowing into the Arctic Ocean.

And yet we have placed upon record but little concerning the natural resources of this big country. From father's letters we readily learn that he valued these resources, and always prophesied a grand future for this, the land of his adoption, and however sanguine his faith, none the less is ours in the solid material worth of this portion of our great Dominion. Our reasons for thus believing are as follows:

1st. *Size.*—From Rat Portage to the summit of the Rocky Mountains, and from the forty-ninth parallel to Great Slave Lake, we have a block 1,000 miles square; beyond this we leave a large margin to be prospected and experimented upon by posterity. Confining ourselves to the above square block, we have an acreage of 640,000,000. Because of swamps and water and unarable parts, let us discount this by half. Mind you, I do not discount any portion; long since I learned to believe that any part of God's creation would eventually fall into line, it being man's mission to discover and utilize. All came from one great Mind. Each is wealthy in its kind. However, deducting half, we have 320,000,000 acres, which would give a population of 3,200,000 souls 100 acres each. No small inheritance this for any people.

2nd. *Climate.*—All over this big stretch of country, spring opens from the first to the twentieth of April, and winter begins from the first to the twentieth of November. Altitude and latitude are such that in the summer season there is very little night, thus there is a large percentage of sun, which to a great extent does away with the probability of frost in summer. Then its situation puts it on the northern slope of the Continent, and thus it is always dropping away from the height of land which lies east and west and south of the forty-ninth parallel. And this fact is to us a very sufficient reason for our not being nearly so subject to storms, blizzards and cyclones in this country as they are in the states and territories south of us. By experience we know that, as other parts of America have been subject to climatic changes consequent upon settlement and occupancy by civilized man, so has this in the portions already thus occupied, and we have no doubt that these changes will multiply as the development and settlement of the country moves on. We believe that nowhere else in the Dominion is there so large a percentage the year round of clear sky and sunshine.

3rd. *Soil.*—Of course, in so vast a territory, there is variety. Light and heavy soils alternate according to geographical position and antecedent conditions. But we believe we are safe in challenging the North American Continent anywhere else to show as much good arable soil per acre as Manitoba and the North-West is possessed of. At Hudson Bay posts and mission stations everywhere in spots through the country, the soil was tested many years since, and the fact practically demonstrated that all the hardier kinds of cereals and roots could be grown, and does not the crop this year satisfy even the most unbeliev-

16

ing as to the possibilities of our western country as a bread producing land.

4th. *The Pasture.*—Here we have one of the largest and best pasture fields in the world. The natural grasses are rich and varied in their quality. In the prairie sections the autumn winds and dry weather, characteristic of that period of the year, cure the grasses and prepare them for winter fodder. Along the base of the mountains there are large sections which are pre-eminently suited for winter ranges. For fifteen winters I have had cattle running at large all the year, with no other provision than that provided by nature. For seventeen years our principal food was buffalo meat, and of course the only food of these animals was the natural pasture to be found all over the North-West. When I first came to the plains, the migrations of these vast herds were north and south ; north in fall and winter, and south in spring and summer. It would take 1,000 railway trains, each carrying 500 head of stock, to move the number of God's cattle I have seen at one time from the summit of one hill by a glance of my naked eye over the country stretching from my feet in every direction. Interspersed among them were thousands of antelope, also feeding upon this big pasture. All these lived and thrived and grew fat without the expenditure of any thought or labor on the part of man; and when, in the order of Divine Providence, these wild animals, having served their purpose, disappeared, they left their immense rich pasture for the occupancy of the economic and thrifty civilized man, who can, if he will, herein raise and graze his flocks and herds away up into the millions in multitude. To-day we have in Manitoba and the North-West, of stock of all kinds, about 350,000 head. At twenty acres per head we have room and pasture for 16,000,-000 head.

5th.   *Water.*—A very small portion of the North-West Territory may be termed arid, and even here there is considerable surface water, and through this the South Saskatchewan flows, and every here and there are to be found living springs, so that what is generally looked upon as the dry portion of our country is not really so, but west and north, and east of this, there is abundance of splendid water.

There are very many small lakes, and the perennial rivers and creeks that flow through the country in every direction are simply " legion."   Among all the big ranges of hills general through the country, but more especially along the immediate base of the mountains, magnificent springs of the finest water are to be found on almost every quarter section.

The drop of the continent to the east and north is such that every stream is a succession of water powers. The rain-fall in the months of June and July is as a rule large, and the dew is also plentiful. Many times have we been wet through and through while hunting stock in the early morn, amid the rank growth of pea vine and blue joint, common to the whole of the Saskatchewan Valley. In twenty-eight years' sojourn north and west of Winnipeg, I have experienced but one season of drouth.

6th. *Minerals.*—That gold, silver, iron, copper, lead and coal form part of the wealth of this country is a well-known fact.

As yet, with the exception of coal, very little has been done towards developing these natural factors in the material advancement of a country. Some placer-digging for gold has been carried on among the bars of the North Saskatchewan and Peace Rivers, and for more than a score of years the sands of the Saskatchewan have been made to yield a revenue to a number of men, who have every spring and fall, with the crudest machinery, washed the glittering gems from the black sands; and though these deposits are continually going on, no one has up to this time found the source. Some day this will be discovered; in the meanwhile quartz leads have been found in the mountains, rich in copper, silver, gold and lead, but the capital for the opening of these has not yet come to the front.   The country is young, and capitalists are careful ; but presently some of the enterprise of the older parts of the world will turn this way, and our mountains and foot-hills will become " hives of industry."

As to coal, it is everywhere.   All the larger rivers, and many of the creeks, cut through and run over beds of " black diamonds."   Both bituminous and anthracite mines are already being worked, and we have no doubt that as railroads penetrate this hitherto wilderness land, the coal industry will assume ·vast proportions.

The states and territories to the south, and our own big prairie section, will need an immense amount of fuel, and here in the North-West we have an unlimited supply of good coal, and the mining and transport of this will furnish employment for thousands in the near future.

I have traced what seems to me to be one immense coal bed from within a few miles of the boundary line to the northern end of Lesser Slave Lake, a distance of 500 miles.

7th. *Timber.*—While Manitoba and the North-West cannot challenge either the Eastern Provinces or

British Columbia in this respect, yet our timber supply is not to be overlooked. With the exception of the most southerly portion, a region of about 400 miles long by 200 miles wide (and in this there are the Moose, Woody, and Cypress Mountains, which are well wooded), all the rest of the country is more or less timbered, prairie and woodland alternating the one with the other everywhere.

The settler, with very little exception, will find on his own homestead fencing and fuel, and material for pioneer buildings, and in many parts he will find himself adjacent to spruce forests, which will attract saw-mills, and thus his lumber supply for the future will be assured. The further north and east one travels the denser is the timber growth, and when settlement and legislation put a stop to prairie fires, this growth will travel southward, for there are valuable kinds of timber indigenous to the soil of the North-West, which only want a chance to grow.

8th. *Appearance.*—This is a land of beauty. There is nothing monotonous about the North-West. The scenery is as varied as the country is large. Here is opportunity for the indulging of every taste. Do you want a flat, even expanse to stand on, a vast level, and let the horizon drop all around you, like unto an inverted bowl? Then Manitoba, from Rat Portage to

Portage la Prairie, and from the boundary line to Lake Winnipeg, will suit you. Would you rather a gently un-undulating land, small hills, broad valleys and graceful slopes? From Portage la Prairie to Calgary, and from the boundary line to Edmonton and Battleford, in a vast area, you have your choice in almost bewildering variety. Do you hanker after water and headland and bay, after gems of islands and labyrinths of intri-cate waterways? Is it music to your ear to listen to the rippling of currents, and tumbling of cascades, and roaring of rapids? Take the country to the north of Rat Portage, and about Norway House and the north shore of Lake Winnipeg, and on, on to Hudson Bay, and westward into the Athabasca country. Here you may paddle and portage "your own canoe" for thou-sands of miles and never need to sigh,

"Oh ! for a lodge in some vast wilderness."

Do you like to ride or drive to the height of some grand range of hills, and from thence look out upon a wondrous panorama of the beauty and variety of God's creation? Come with me to the Nose, or Eye, or Ear, or Sickness Hills, ranging along in distances from the South Branch northward to the Saskatche-wan, and from the summit of any one of these your eye will reach out forty and fifty miles in every direc-tion, and will gradually accustom itself to taking in

the rich landscape scenery which in grand profusion
is before us.

Hills and valleys, shapely as they have fallen from
Nature's lathe.   Islands of timber and fields of prairie,
artistically arranged, and so placed that however cultivated your taste, you would not change them if you
could.   Glistening lakelets and winding creeks, "like
threads of silver" intersperse the scene.   In season
the smell of rank vegetation, and the aroma of thousands of wild rose beds, is wafted to your nostrils, and
to crown all, you expand your lungs and breathe a
most glorious atmosphere ; for you are on the Highlands of America and in the garden of the Dominion,
and strange to say, that, as yet, from any one of these
high places I have mentioned, you will look in vain
for the smoke from a settler's chimney, for up to the
time of my writing none have reached thus far.

Perhaps you crave something vaster, grander, more
majestic still ; let us stand on one of the ranges of
hills running north and south, about 150 miles east
of the base of the Rocky Mountains ; if the day is
clear and bright, we will look upon a painting worth
making an effort to behold.   Yonder, rising range
beyond range, and stretching north and south and
giving us the compass of an immense region, are
the Grand Mountains,

"Where to cloudland and glory
God transfigures the sod."

The forests as they climb the steeps and the perpendicular rocks as they stand heavenward darken the
scene, but above them the snow-clad fields and glaciers,
that never melt, glisten in the sun. Perhaps, as we
look, a fleecy cloud catches on some peaks, and for a
little veils these from our vision, or lower down a
thunder-storm rolls up against the mountains, and
while we see the lightning and hear the distant roar
of thunder above the dark cloud, we see the summits
shining with reflected rays, unmoved and unnerved by
the force of electric shock and storm upon their sides.

Let us draw nearer, and presently we begin to notice
the Foot Hills. Like many an æsthetic Christian, we
had been looking above, and missed seeing the beauties
and duties of lower life. Now these great hills attract
our attention, their wooded slopes and summits finely
shaded by Douglass and spruce trees, with the prairie
sod growing in among their roots, strike us as very
gems of picnic grounds. Take the Foot Hills from
the Old Man River to the Athabasca, and they rival
the most perfect natural scenery. Here we have
mountains, prairie, woodland, river, lake, all harmon-
iously blended by nature, into a great, grand and ever-
changing picture.

Going into the mountains, we find that they are not all rock and snow, but that intersecting them everywhere there are charming valleys and thousands of ready-made camping grounds, and an infinitude of streams and lakes, all more or less full of fish, so that for years we might spend the whole summer, and by changing our routes, always have fresh fields and scenes.

Just one thought more. When you hear any one say, "I know all about the North-West," please discount that statement; do so largely, for no man living knows all about this great, big, wonderful land. Geological, geographical and botanical surveys may continue for years to come (and it is proper they should), but after all "the half will not have been told."

My opportunity has been a good one, perhaps better than that of any living white man, especially as to what is termed "the Fertile Belt," and yet I am free to confess, I know but little. The field is so large, the problem so great, it will take time to discover and solve; but here let me place on record that I firmly believe in the capability of this part of our great Dominion for the maintenance of a large population, which will be in no wise disappointed in the heritage God has reserved for them.

J. McDougall.

Morley, *April 6th, 1888.*

www.ingramcontent.com/pod-product-compliance
Lightning Source LLC
Chambersburg PA
CBHW030816020726
47499CB00006B/1948